RAINY DAYS, SUNNY DAYS
SATURDAY'S CHILD

BY DEBORAH CHURCHMAN AND ANNE H. OMAN

Illustrations by Becky Heavner

WASHINGTON BOOK TRADING COMPANY

Published by the Washington Book Trading Company.
Copyright 1987 by Deborah Churchman and Anne H. Oman.
Illustrations copyright 1987 by The Washington Book Trading Company.
All rights reserved. No part of this publication may be reproduced without prior written permission of the publisher.
ISBN 0915168111 $6.95

The Washington Book Trading Company
P.O. Box 1676, Arlington, Virginia 22210
Nancy Carter Modrak, Editor
Keren Ruth Modrak, Editorial Assistant
Ed Schneider, Designer
Composition by Wordscape

This book is dedicated, with great affection, to our children and to the editors, past and present, of the Weekend section of the *Washington Post*, who made all these excursions possible.

Deborah Churchman, a native Washingtonian and former researcher at National Geographic, writes family and education articles for the *Washington Post, Christian Science Monitor*, and *New York Times*. Her four children have assisted her on countless forays for the Weekend section of the *Washington Post*.

Anne H. Oman, a Washington-based writer and former assistant editor of National Geographic *World*, has three daughters who have grown up on assignment for the Weekend section of the *Washington Post*.

Rainy Days 9
Gallivanting at Galleries 10
Art-Full Opportunities 14
Rubbing Up the Past at the Cathedral 20
The World in the Cathedral Windows 24
Computers Kids Can Do 28
Exploring the High C's 34
Living in the Past 39
Reading Up a Summer Storm 41
Saturday Music Lessons for a Song 47
Behind the Food Scene 50
Feeding Time in the Shark Tank 55
Rolling Along at the Rinks 58
Learning Labs at the Zoo 65
Truly Little Theatre 69
Seeing How Others See 74

Sunny Days 79
Finding the Summer Camps 80
Ambushing Your Own Great Pumpkin 85
The Horses of Fort Myer 89
Grounds for Play 92
Hiking with Half-Pints 100
Touring with Tots: A Potpourri of Places 106
Aboard the USS Barry 113
Digging Up the Past 117
Cruising Clopper Lake 122
Wave Pools: Surf on Tap 126

Feeding the Ducks **132**
Exploring an Estuary **136**
A Swamp with Knees **140**
Tame Ways to the Wild **142**
Birding for Beginners **146**
Historic Farms **151**

Saturday's Child 157
A Civil War Tour for Families **158**
Rose Hill Manor: Hands-on History **164**
Small Fry at the Trout Hatchery **168**
America's High Flying Past **172**
Visiting Maryland Farms **177**
Finding Fossils at Calvert Cliffs **180**
Lights Fantastic: Beacons on the Bay **183**
Setting Sail for the Maritime Museum **186**
On the Beach, By the Bay **189**
The Real Live Little Ponies **194**
The Famous Wild Ponies **198**
The Still-Enchanted Forest **202**
Up, Around, and In a Wonderful Waterfall **206**

INTRODUCTION

Children are a great excuse for going on outings, and being a reporter is a great excuse for asking a lot of questions.

To write the articles in this book, we combined our roles as parents and journalists. We took our children—a total of seven—to attractions all around the Washington area, and we brought along our reporters' notebooks. We tried to ask the questions we thought other parents might want to ask and since we were often permitted to go behind the scenes, we tried to add information that will make our readers' rainy days, sunny days, and Saturdays more enjoyable.

We have omitted some of the most popular attractions, such as the Smithsonian Museums and the excellent Capital Children's Museum, on the grounds that you already know about them. Instead, we've focused on attractions and opportunities you might not know about. And we've been very sure to include the ones our own children liked the best—as well as answers to the questions they had and such practical information as whether a hiking trail will take a stroller.

As parents to parents, we wish you happy exploring.

RAINY DAYS

GALLIVANTING AT THE GALLERIES

n the water floats a naked young man, eyes rolled up in panic, arms flailing, his right leg crunched off at the knee and trailing blood. Lunging just inches from his head is what looks like the designer model for Jaws IV—a gleaming-toothed monster shark, malice rippling through its frenzied body.

The guy in the water is a goner, for sure.

But wait! Next to him (heart-rendingly out of reach) is a boat manned by sailors intent on rescuing our hero. Two stretch out their arms; one

flings a rope; another aims grimly with a harpoon at the shark below.

Will the rescue come in time? And even if the harpoonist slays this shark, what about that menacing fin behind him? Could the oarsman steer close enough for rescue before the victim loses his head?

Welcome to the wonderful world of art.

"Kids love this painting. You can't get them away from it," says Lynn Russell at the National Gallery of Art, which offers art appreciation tours by reservation on most Saturdays for families with children aged 6 to 12. "I always start by asking them what's going to happen, and usually we figure that there's no way he'll be rescued; the shark is just too close."

In fact, she says, spilling the beans, the man in the water, Brook Watson, was saved. He commissioned the painting by John Singleton Copley in the late eighteenth century.

The painting serves as a good tool for teaching things like balance (why is the shark in the middle of the painting?), line (why is everyone placed in a zig-zag pattern?), and color (what feeling do these cold colors convey?). And it serves Russell's larger goal: helping folks learn how to really use their eyes.

People don't know how to notice things, she says, "which is one of the reasons we have all this ugly architecture around. Most people grow up visually crippled."

She's out to change all that by training children

(and their parents) how to "really look at a painting. This doesn't depend on something they've studied in the classroom or how smart they are; it's all right in front of them."

Kids are good at this sort of observing, she says, "though they haven't been trained in how to express their visual knowledge. I'll ask them a question and they'll tell me, 'It's that guy over there in the picture,' and I'll have to keep pulling at them until they say, 'It's the guy in the red bathing suit next to the beach towel.'"

In front of George Bellows' boxing painting, "Both Members of This Club," she'll ask who's going to win the fight depicted, and why. "The 'why' tells you how the child is thinking and what he's noticing," she says.

She likes to draw children to the little clues in a painting that contribute to its feeling. One of Bellows' boxers—the clear loser—has a red face, "and some kid will always say, 'He got his face smashed in,'" she says. "Then I'll ask them what the color red reminds them of, and eventually somebody will say blood and pain. Then they'll see that Bellows was trying to show the pain of that moment."

She encourages the kids to play with line, like the curves that wave through Mary Cassatt's "The Boating Party." "I ask them what curving lines like this," she says, her arms flowing languidly through the air, "make them feel like, and they usually decide it's relaxing, like you feel at the beach."

Around sculpture she tries to get the audience to

think like sculptors, asking them, "What's the first thing you have to do when you've got this block of marble?" They'll settle on a subject—a child, perhaps—and then she'll ask, "What should you have in front of you before you start? First they'll say, 'A photograph of a boy,' and we'll have to discuss what they did in the days before photography."

"Then you'll get this, 'ooo, ooo' with kids waving their arms in the air, and one will say, 'A child!' "

This kind of reasoning is easy to learn and adds a depth to the viewing of any work of art, Russell believes. "People really are perceptive, if you guide them a little," she says. "And we hope they'll see with a little practice that they can learn to do it by themselves."

Once you learn to see, though, museums can be a real vision.

Art Tours
• *Family tours at the National Gallery of Art (Constitution Avenue at 6th Street N.W., Washington) are given most Saturdays throughout the year. Christmas tours, starting in December, are probably the most popular. Groups have individual instructors and average no more than about 20 persons. Reservations required; phone 842-6249.*
• *The Phillips Collection (1600 21st Street N.W., Washington) offers occasional family-designed tours with their special exhibits; phone 387-0961 for more information.*

ART-FULL OPPORTUNITIES

When the 8- to 10-year-olds in Patti Koreski's class on Masterpieces at the Corcoran did Picasso, she had them drawing on each other's faces with eyeliner pencils "to break the faces into pieces, like a puzzle," she says. Rousseau's whimsical tiger was the inspiration for child-crafted animal masks; and for Van Gogh, the kids imitated his swirling colors after listening to the song "Vincent."

"We use different gimmicks to show off different techniques," says Koreski, an art teacher in the Fairfax Public Schools who spends her Saturdays with children at the Corcoran. "If you can involve their bodies, it's better than just the visual—they understand more," she thinks.

It's an approach that works well with these children, talented youngsters who willingly give up precious Saturday mornings to, as Phillip Panusz (age 9¾) puts it, "make my art better."

It's a goal shared by all his fellow students, kids who drive in the from the 'burbs with their folks or arrive in limos from the local embassies. Art classes don't come cheap, and parents who might shell out bucks for a year of piano lessons, regardless of talent, don't tend to sign their children up for drawing unless the kid veers that way. The Bethesda youth, Phillip, points to the things all these kids have in common: "I draw all the time," he confides.

The Corcoran is one of the best—and most expensive—places to take a child like Phillip. Teachers there understand both the medium and the method, know how to make art approachable for young children and workable for teens, and seem to genuinely enjoy their charges. "Some of my hardest working students are the high school kids," says Dennis O'Neil, who teaches a printmaking class on Saturdays.

For O'Neil, the criterion for giving a child this kind of opportunity shouldn't be talent, but enthusiasm. "If someone's enthusiastic about art, we can teach him regardless of talent," he says. "The reverse is not true."

Other teachers agree: "If a student loves art, he's going to find a way to get this kind of class whether his parents arrange it or not," says Franklin White, whose Saturday class at the Corcoran helps students develop a portfolio to show to prospective colleges.

But Susan Framberg, who helps organize the Art Barn's children's classes, believes discipline is the key. She thinks all children can learn to appreciate the techniques and visual messages of art if they're exposed to it, and worries a bit that only the "arty" kids get the lessons and trips to the art gallery that foster this kind of appreciation.

She gives this example: "Parents brought a boy here who just hated it the first week, and didn't like it the second week," she says. "But by the third week, he really enjoyed it, and kept coming back. Sometimes, it's just a matter of trying," she thinks.

Once you and your child have decided to give art classses a try, you have to track down a good teacher. Just like finding a good music class, it ain't as easy as it looks.

Anne Thomas, executive director of the Greater Reston Arts Center, gives this advice: "Try to find teachers who are trained both as artists and educators. Sometimes you'll find someone who really knows his medium but doesn't know how to communicate that knowledge," she says.

She also thinks students "need opportunities for individual development. The teacher shouldn't say, 'Here's a still life; we're all going to do it and it should look this way.' On the other hand," she says, "they shouldn't just say, 'Here are the materials; have fun.' "

You're pretty much guaranteed quality and a mix of creativity and technique at a professional school like the Corcoran. But before you shell out the dollars—and subject your child to lessons she may not be able to sit still for—you might like to try out a less high-powered art experience.

The Art Barn is the perfect place for this sort of trial. The two-hour Saturday sessions are free for 6- to 12-year-olds, though they ask for a $1 donation, and teachers change from week to week.

The Art Barn shows a different medium each month; those displaying their work are expected to teach one of these Saturday classes. That means your child will be learning from someone who makes their professional living in that medium.

"It took me a long time to figure this out," says Ina Schetor, explaining how to get a blurry or sharp effect from the watercolors in front of the dozen girls and boys she taught recently at the Art Barn, "so if you pay attention, you'll save yourself a lot of trouble." By the time she was through, the kids had moved from tentative, gradeschool watercolors to a painterly, creative approach—turning out eight or ten paintings on the way.

The next step up may be a class run by your local recreation department. Parents give varying critiques to these experiences, which tend to weigh heavily on the artsy-craftsy end of art. But some county classes feature things the Art Barn simply can't duplicate, like potter's wheels, darkrooms, and printmaking equipment. Getting to use the equipment is worth the cost of the class, and (if the parents are to be believed) you may stumble across some truly talented teachers.

Local art guilds are another place to find classes for children. Places like the Capitol Hill Arts Workshop and the Greater Reston Arts Center offer everything from drawing to paper sculpture, all for roughly $3 to $5 per teaching hour. Reston uses art educators as teachers, and can give your school-age child in-depth exposure to drawing technique.

That leaves places like the Corcoran, the Art League (at the Torpedo Factory in Alexandria), and the Maryland College of Art and Design in Silver Spring for children and teens who are, as one instructor put it, "serious about art—this isn't babysitting." Many, though not most, of these students go on to major in art; White says a few of his students "grew up at the Corcoran."

Evi Westmore, an 11-year-old from Falls Church taking the Corcoran's Junior Studies program, says she likes it because "the other kids in class are serious about art. In some other art classes I've taken," she says, "people goof around."

She and other students say they also enjoy having access to materials and equipment unavailable in their local classes. "And I like going downtown," she says. "I enjoy that."

Whether it's downtown or across the street, all these schools have one goal: To turn on and train the talent. And if you look carefully, chances are you can find a trainer to match your talented trainee.

Getting into Art
Washington
* *Art Barn, 2401 Tilden Street, N.W., 426-6719. Free classes for children on Saturdays from 10 to 12.*
* *Capitol Hill Arts Workshop, 545 7th Street, S.E., 547-6839. Afterschool and Saturday classes include crafts, mixed art, pottery, drawing and painting for children aged 5 to 14.*
* *Corcoran School of Art, 17th Street and New York Avenue, N.W., 628-9484. Many media taught to children aged 6 to adult.*

Maryland
* *Glen Echo Park, MacArthur Boulevard, Glen*

Echo, 492-6282. A few art classes for kids; more for adults.

* *Maryland College of Art and Design, 10500 Georgia Avenue, Silver Spring, 649-4454. Saturday classes for kids 14 and older include drawing and painting. Students taught the same as we teach our degree students, says a spokesman.*

Virginia

* *Art League, 105 North Union Street, Alexandria, 683-2323. Classes for 4-year-olds to adult, year round.*
* *Greater Reston Arts Center, 11400 Washington Plaza West, Reston, 471-9242. Classes for 8- to 14-year-olds include drawing, painting, paper sculpture, and printmaking.*
* *Springfield Art Guild, 7058 Spring Garden Drive, Brookfield Plaza, Springfield, 451-7287. Saturday and Monday classes for children aged 8 to 17 concentrate on drawing, with some watercolor.*

RUBBING UP THE PAST AT THE CATHEDRAL

"We call her the lace lady, even though her dress was really brocade and velvet," explains Ann Etches of the London Brass Rubbing Centre in the nether regions of Washington Cathedral. Eleven-year-old Elizabeth and her sister Katherine, 9, want to do rubbings of one Margaret Peyton, who put on her best dress and had her image cast in brass back in the 1400s. But since only one brass image of Peyton—copied from a larger original in a church in Cambridgeshire—is available at the time, Etches diplomatically tries to interest Katherine in another subject.

"That's Henry Stafford," she says, pointing to a brass knight. "He's bigger; there's a lot of rubbing for small fingers there. But he has nice armor, hasn't he?"

After inspecting dozens of knights, ladies, religious scenes, and animals, Katherine decides on another fifteenth century woman, Margaret Spycer.

Etches approves the choice, noting that the brass figure has distinctly raised edges, which makes for a well-defined rubbing, and that it's not so big that a child will tire of the work before it's finished.

"Brass rubbing became the fashion in the thirteenth century, shortly after brass was invented, and died in the sixteenth century. We don't know why it went out of fashion, but it came into fashion again in the beginning of this century. Most of the subjects were quite ordinary examples of their class, knights and their ladies and wool merchants and some ecclesiastical gentlemen and lawyers. Their portraits were placed on the floors of small medieval churches."

After being walked on for centuries, many church brasses are in such bad shape that church authorities don't allow them to be rubbed. So the London Brass Rubbing Centre has made copies of them. Some are exact-size replicas, made by taking a wax mold of the original, building it up with epoxy resin, and putting brass on top. Some are copies, smaller than the originals. The Centre pays annual royalties to churches that let them make reproductions of their brasses, and these royalties help keep many churches going, Etches says.

To get the girls started, she tapes 100 percent rag paper tautly over the brasses. Katherine's paper is black, but Elizabeth, despite a warning that it's hard to erase your mistakes on white paper, chooses white.

"First, you take a piece of cloth with your fingers and rub it over the outlines of the brass to mark them on the paper," she tells them. Then she lets the kids pick out pieces of beeswax, which have metal resins in them and come in metallic colors. Using the side of the wax, the girls trace the outline of the brass.

"Now take the shoulder of the wax—the curved part—and make short hard, up-and-down strokes over the whole brass, always going in the same direction," she instructs. "When you're finished with that, you'll want me again."

"It's just like doing a leaf, but a little more complicated," says Elizabeth.

"I've rubbed pennies," says Katherine.

Armed with such experience, the girls proceed to rub, using pieces of cardboard to keep their wax from going outside the lines.

"Is 1442 the year she was born?" asks Katherine. "No," replies Etches, "that was the year the brass image was made."

"She looks tired," remarks Elizabeth. "I guess she had to stand still a long time."

In about fifteen minutes, the portraits are completed and the girls polish them with cloths. All around them in every cranny of the cathedral crypt, people are rubbing. An adult is rolling up a life-size rubbing of a knight. A 5-year-old is completing a presentable rubbing of a lamb.

"The animals were taken from the bottom of the brasses," explains Etches. "Men were often pictured with a lion, the symbol of courage, while women were often pictured with a dog, the symbol of faithfulness."

Etches removes the paper from the brasses, and the girls erase their stray marks.

"We don't really know who did the brasses," says Etches. "They were illiterate people, generally, and couldn't have signed their names. Do you notice how many of the knights have their legs crossed? It was once thought that this meant they had been successful in the Crusades. But a historian did some research and found that many of the knights had never gone to the Crusades. It was simply a more comfortable pose."

There's the Rub
• *The London Brass Rubbing Centre is located in the Crypt Gift Shop of Washington Cathedral, Wisconsin and Massachusetts Avenues, N.W., Washington. The charge for rubbing includes materials and depends on the brass selected. For information call 364-0030.*

THE WORLD IN THE CATHEDRAL WINDOWS

We went to see some cartoons the other day that were showing in full color. They weren't Disney, but the stories were great, the characters were deep and wonderful, and the lighting was fantastic.

A "cartoon" in the medieval sense is the design used for stained glass windows, "comic books" for illiterate congregations in cathedrals throughout Europe of that day. At the Washington Cathedral the same gothic style has been going up since 1907, filled with literally hundreds of these "comics."

There you can find a window depicting industrial and social reformers like Nehemiah (by Napoleon A. Setti); another showing architects like Solomon (by Albert Birkle); and another depicting educators from Plato and St. Paul to Horace Mann (by Wilbur H. Burnham). There are windows of healing, humanitarianism, and freedom, and a space window showing the first moon landing with a piece of the rock pinioned in the middle (by Rodney Winfield).

And, of course, there are religious windows. One shows Jesus as a child playing ball. Another, Rowan LeCompte's magnificent West Rose Window, is an abstract design showing a gathering of light and energy illustrating the account in

Genesis of God's creation of the universe.

We went to the Cathedral's gift shop to find a book describing each window. After looking through this for ideas, the children used onion-skin typing paper to make their own cartoons.

First, they drew designs in black pen and colored them in with crayons. Then we rubbed the finished product with a light film of vegetable oil (to make the paper even more translucent) and taped our designs to the window for a lovely effect.

By this time we felt sure enough about our designing prowess to try a more tactile approach: Stained Glass Cookies made from a recipe in Evelyn Coskey's *Christmas Crafts for Everyone*. Using ropes of cookie dough "lead," we fashioned our cartoons. These we filled with crushed hard candies that melted in the oven to become our "glass."

I suppose we could have lacquered the cookies to become "sun catchers" or next year's Christmas tree ornaments, but we all found a more mouthwatering solution to their disposal. Here's the recipe:

Stained Glass Cookies

¾ cup shortening softened (or part butter, part shortening)

1 cup sugar

2 eggs

1 teaspoon vanilla

½ teaspoon lemon extract

2½ cups all-purpose flour

1 teaspoon baking powder

1 teaspoon salt
6 packages candy mints, or 1 pound sour balls, peppermint candies or lollipops, crushed

Cream the sugar and shortening together; beat in the eggs with the extracts. Mix together the flour, baking powder, and salt, and stir this mixture into the shortening a little at a time. You may need to add more flour to make the dough manageable, depending on how humid the day is.

Evelyn Coskey's book has a three-page description of how to make the cookies; here's what we learned. Cover your cookie sheets with a layer of aluminum foil. Flour your hands and, working with a pinch at a time, roll the dough out into very thin coils (they spread in the oven). Form the coils into shapes, leaving large holes.

Fill the holes with crushed candies (we broke ours with a hammer between two sheets of waxed paper). You may use one color for each hole, or mix colors for a mottled effect—ours did not blend, for some reason. Try to keep the layer of crushed candies even so your "glass" will be smooth.

When the first cookie sheet is full, bake in a preheated 375 degree oven for seven to nine minutes, or until the cookie dough is starting to harden (it does not turn brown until past done). Remove the sheet, and allow the cookies to cool completely before removing them from the foil. We did not find it necessary to grease the foil beforehand.

This batch made a little over four sheets of cookie designs for us.

Stained Glass Window Tours
• *Washington Cathedral, Wisconsin and Massachusetts Avenues, N.W., Washington, 537-6200. Tours, which point out several windows, take 30 to 45 minutes and start at the west end near the Wisconsin Avenue entrance. Call for schedule.*
• *Evelyn Coskey's Christmas Crafts for Everyone* was published by Abingdon Press in 1976, $9.95.

COMPUTERS KIDS CAN DO

Do you have a computer at home? Bought it for the kids, huh? Bet they're tired of those two programs you bought them that looked really good in the store and were practically guaranteed to teach them reading or at least math by now, right?

Oh, you don't have a computer at home? What are you, some kind of communist? You say you're thinking of buying it (for the kids), but are still sorting through your options?

Well, hey, check this out—kids can do computers at the library. If you live in Arlington, Montgomery, or Prince George's County,

Alexandria, or the District, you can send the kids (or go with them) to the library and let them wear their little fingers down to the bone making computer-designed cards, matching computer-graphics dinosaurs, or programming a face to stick out its tongue at you—with sound effects.

Most of this is done on Apple IIe computers, but the libraries managed to afford all those options you wanted—a mouse, a printer, and (in Arlington, at least) a koala pad. And all the libraries have more programs than even the most indulgent parent would think of owning.

It's all available free to those willing to attend a brief workshop (in Arlington and Potomac), run through a self-training program (in Alexandria and Prince George's County), or just plough in (in the District). Kids are asked to sign up by grade level in all the suburbs. In Arlington, pre-schoolers are invited to use the terminals with the aid of their parents.

"It's funny to see the difference in learning styles between adults and children," says Kristy Beavin, librarian in charge of computers at Arlington. "The kids just rush right in, hit any key; the parents want to know exactly what they're supposed to do—they're much less willing to experiment. So, of course, the kids learn faster," she says.

Workshops we attended in Arlington and Potomac demonstrated the computer, showing participants how to turn it on and get the programs working. Librarians also described and demonstrated some of the broad range of software available, everything from spread sheets and electronic mail systems at Potomac to the ever popular "Facemaker" and "Dinosaurs" in Arlington.

"Our programs are in that squishy area between education and arcade," says Beavin. Aimed at kids and their parents ("pre-schoolers are our heaviest users," she says), Arlington's computer access program has already trained 600 users for the Apple IIe at the Central library. Beavin moved on to the Columbia Pike Branch in Arlington, where she developed a more adult-oriented computer system, she says.

Alexandria, which has had public access computing for four years, has signed up "over 1,000 users," says librarian Deborah Reinfried. Using a computer at the library appears to be a growing thing nationally and a very popular thing locally. "Our schedule is usually 75 to 100 percent full," says Beavin of Arlington, where patrons can sign up in advance for a half hour per week.

The extensive use points to library dollars well spent, she thinks. "A very popular book in the children's room will circulate perhaps six times per year. Our most popular software will circulate 15 times per week," says Beavin.

Parents sometimes use the library as a way to preview software before buying it, Beavin reports. "We've been surprised to find that some of these people have PCs at home, but they come in here to try out our programs."

What they find, says Marsha Thessin of Arlington, parent of Rachel, 5, is that "she plays with the games for a couple of weeks, but it's the educational ones she comes back to over and over again."

Although the suburban libraries have deliberately bought the same type of computer as their school systems own, they tend to stay away from curriculum-type software. In that way they're very different from the public access computer system at the Martin Luther King Library downtown.

There, young adults aged 12 to 19 have their own computer lab where they can hone educational skills from math to language arts. "It comes through a modem from our main database," says librarian Michael Wallace. "There are eight terminals, so there's usually no waiting. But we run 40 to 70 young people in here per day in the summer."

The King library programs "give immediate feedback to the young person and work with him at his own pace," Wallace says. Only those young adults with a library card can use the system, he says, "and we've found that people are coming here and getting a card just to use the system."

Presumably, all those D.C. library patrons are using the computer to get a leg up on their schoolwork. But Lynn Hough, computer librarian at the Potomac library, thinks there's simply a fascination with computers among children. "We train the adults, and then the kids wander over and want to know how it works and what it can do." she says.

The kids have found that when it comes to computers, the library's the place to check it out.

Where the Computers Are
Virginia

• *Ellen Coolidge Burke Branch, 4701 Seminary Road, Alexandria, 370-6050. Apple II Plus, and over 40 programs available for children 4 and up. Patrons must run through the Apple Introduces Apple program before gaining access. Until they can read, pre-schoolers must be accompanied by parents. Variable hours.*

• *James M. Duncan, Jr. Branch, 2501 Commonwealth Avenue, Alexandria, 838-4566. Apple IIe, printer, and about 30 programs available for adults and children age 4 and up. See above for rules.*

• *Central Library, 1015 North Quincy Street, Arlington, 284-8181, Apple IIe with printer, mouse, and koala pad, available in children's room. Children in first to eighth grade must attend workshop; parents attend workshop for preschooler. Computer available ½ hour per week; advance sign-up. Eighty programs, from Stickybear to Printshop. Hours: 9 to 9, Monday through Thursday; Sunday, 1 to 9.*

• *Columbia Pike Branch, 816 South Walter Reed Drive, Arlington, 553-2323. Computer access for children and adults available; see above for rules.*

Washington

• *Martin Luther King Memorial Library, 901 G Street, N.W., 727-5535. Computer Lab available in Young Adult section for people aged 12 to 19 years with a library card. Twenty-five programs offer drill and instruction in math, English, high*

school equivalency, and other academic subjects. Computer available in 45-minute slots; register when you arrive. Eight terminals. Variable hours.
Maryland
• *Potomac Library, 10000 Falls Road, Potomac, 365-0662. Apple IIe, Macintosh, printer, mouse and 100 programs available to those who've taken their workshop, given twice every Thursday evening (sign up in advance). Software is oriented toward adults but includes some children's items, like Stickybear. Can reserve up to two hours per week. Variable hours.*
• *Prince George's County. Each branch offering computer access has an IBM PC, Apple IIe, and Macintosh, complete with printers and one to two dozen pieces of software. The software is chiefly for adults, although there are some educational programs children might enjoy. Patrons must sign a user agreement card and run through a tutorial program for each computer type. Youths 16 and under must sign up with parents' permission; kids 8 and under can use the computers only with a parent watching. The branches with computers are: Hillcrest Heights, 2398 Iverson Street, Temple Hills, 630-4900. Laurel, 507 7th Street, Laurel, 776-6790. New Carrollton, 7414 Riversdale Road, New Carrollton, 459-6900. Hours at the branches vary.*

EXPLORING THE HIGH C'S

When opera singers open their mouths for kids, the performers know what to expect: children asking the strangest things.

"They want to know if the sword is real," says soprano Denise Freeland (no, they use a blunted one to prevent any on-stage accidents), "and how we can sing that high" (it takes practice).

Then again, during one of Freeland's frequent visits to schools, a child "asked very seriously how singing opera fits in with the rest of our lives, and

how our friends feel about it. And in every audience," she says, "there's at least one child who wants to learn to sing as a career, and their parents want to know how to encourage it."

Children generally have little trouble relating to opera, and sort out the good and bad guys and their tricks and schemes quickly, once they get used to the fact that everything is sung.

The Opera Theatre of Northern Virginia, which sends a pre-show kit to school groups attending its performances, offers this caution: "When we see a motion picture, we accept without a thought that we see a character in New York on a Tuesday afternoon, and 15 seconds later we see him in Paris, supposedly two weeks later. Opera presents a new sort of illusion that the viewer needs to become accustomed to."

The illusion, the Theatre says, is based on a "natural characteristic of speech"—its musical quality. "Try saying 'good morning' four different ways, as if you were in four very different moods, and listen to the pitch levels of your voice," they suggest.

The Opera Theatre also offers this advice: once your children receive the stunning news that everything—everything—is sung in opera, and try singing everything themselves for a while (please pass the salt, tra la), you might then want to work in a little explanation of some of the conventions of opera.

When someone sings alone ("aria"), you might want to tell them, he's probably telling either the audience or someone else in the cast how he feels about the story at that point. If two or more characters decide to describe these feelings, it's called an "ensemble." And if a character or two or three or more want to move the plot along, it's a "recitative."

Opera Theatre warns children that they're not supposed to be able to understand what each character is saying when everyone sings at once. The melodies of the individual singers should convey the mood, however, and operas for children are notoriously good at body language.

"There's lots of movement," says Freeland, "because there has to be. The little kids sit right down in front, and we can tell instantly if we've lost their attention. So we do a lot of broad comedy, a lot of slapstick."

Then, if members of the audience still have questions, the company urges them to stay afterward "for as long as it takes to answer everyone's questions—that's the best part," says Freeland. "Then we find out what they really thought of it."

Getting into Life on the High C's
• *Opera Theatre of Northern Virginia offers a children's opera in late fall, usually held at the Thomas Jefferson Community Theater, 125 South Old Glebe Road, Arlington. For information phone 739-2918.*

LIVING IN THE PAST

"**H**ow did you children get here this morning?" asks the storyteller at Colvin Run Mill of a group of 15 children, from 4 to 6 years old. "Did you come by car, bus, or truck?"

"I came by a green Datsun," answers Alan, age 5.

The storyteller takes this in stride and proceeds to describe a remarkably similar little boy named Willie whose mode of transportation was a wagon and a horse. Willie, in this nineteenth century tale, takes a trip to a blacksmith shop and receives a gift of a hammered horseshoe nail for accomplishing that most difficult task: sitting still.

It's a task many of the children present find impossible to perform, so the wigglers are trooped outdoors to visit the park's blacksmith corner where they're allowed to touch both horseshoe and nail. They also visit the park's nineteenth century mill, where puppets popping out of boxes, grindstones, and doorways explain what life was like during its heyday.

During the summer, several such tours are offered, transporting area children into the nineteenth century world of Colvin Run Mill and the Clara Barton House, or the eighteenth century days of Sully Plantation and Alexandria.

Most of these programs book early, so if you hit

the phones in the spring, by the end of summer your children could have a feel for the games, crafts, and chores of their peers in earlier centuries.

Chores are the focus at Colvin Run Mill, where 7- to 12-year-olds learn what it was like to be a miller's apprentice. "They'll sharpen the stone, weigh the grain, and thresh and clean the wheat," says a mill spokeswoman.

Wait a minute. Does she really think that the average school-age child, the one who won't clean his room, is going to clean wheat? Just how is she going to get these kids to work? "Well, it's a game here, not something they'd usually do at home." Long pause. "And we'll play real games—blindman's bluff, hoops, things like that."

Hoops are also featured at a program run by Sully Plantation called Become an 18th-Century Child. For four hours, children 10 to 12 learn quilling (a paper craft), stenciling, eighteenth century songs accompanied by an autoharp player, and Prisoner's Base, a line game similar to Red Rover. Then they cook dessert in the kitchen and picnic on the plantation's spacious grounds.

These newly taught eighteenth century experts will fit in well at Tavern Days, held in Gadsby's Tavern in August, where "life in an eighteenth century tavern" is recreated with food and drink, demonstrations, music and special activities for children.

The program promises such things as making a tavern sign, handling eighteenth century artifacts, bed-roping, and the drinking of Twitchell, a molasses-based drink that must be an acquired taste.

For those whose tastes run more toward arts and crafts, the Clara Barton House next to Glen Echo gives a Victorian crafts program for 8- to 12-year-olds.

But more than arts and crafts transcend the generations of childhood. Take the case of James, age 5, who came to Colvin Run Mill to study early nineteenth century life along with the other kids. His examination was a little closer than most, for toward the end of the puppet show he tugged on the sleeve of guide Evelyn Williams and pointed solemnly to his shoeless foot.

The missing item turned up in the mill mechanism, and James with an animal cracker in one hand and a paper-cutout wagon in the other, left with the memory of an incident that surely must have happened to a number of nineteenth century children.

Childhood Past Times
Virginia

• *Colvin Run Mill, Fairfax, 759-2771. Programs for preschoolers and school-age children given throughout the year using puppets, stories, crafts, chores, and games. Fees.*

• *Sully Plantation, Chantilly, 437-1794. Programs for school-age children during the summer; school classes and Scout troops during the year. Admission.*

• *Gadsby's Tavern, Old Town Alexandria,*

838-4242. Tavern Days the second week in August for ages 5 and up; includes crafts, demonstrations, music, and foods of eighteenth century tavern. Fee.
* *Woodlawn Plantation, Mount Vernon, 557-7881. An early eighteenth century house down the road from Mount Vernon has a room of children's toys (dollhouse, rockinghorse, dancing dolls, and wooden toys) available for youngsters to play with. Open daily 9:30 to 4. Fee.*

Maryland

* *Clara Barton House, Glen Echo, 492-6246. Summer programs teach Victorian crafts and games.*
* *Rose Hill Children's Museum. See Rose Hill Manor chapter below.*

READING UP A SUMMER STORM

Here comes the summer and the annual sacrifice of children's bodies and minds to roller coasters, wave pools, and the hot glare of MTV. But just because they're throwing down school books doesn't mean they have to throw over the joys of reading, does it?

"Children who like to read usually read more in the summer," says Fairfax County Librarian Elizabeth Quay. "And children who normally only pick up books because of school assignments can be persuaded to read for fun in the summer because the pressure is off."

Oh, yeah? And just how, short of wiring the kid to the word processor, does one do that?

"There are a lot of ways to pique a child's interest in books besides shoving a book under her nose," says Maria Salvadore, D.C. children's librarian.

One of the best is to bring her to places where librarians such as Salvadore hawk their wares—the local library. There, experts in children's literature are waiting to steer, nudge, and encourage your child's reading habits.

Starting early in summer, most library systems in the area dangle lures—movies, storytelling, computers, puppets, and live animals—to get kids where the books are.

In Fairfax County, children sign up and receive a pamphlet ("Think of it as a passport," says Quay) with their name on the back. As they finish a book, they come to the library and write its title and author in their booklet, and fill in the blank with (Oh, boy!) a sticker, one for each of eight different categories. A book of jokes, for instance, earns them a "Giggles" sticker; reading "The Hobbit" or one of Lloyd Alexander's fantasies earns an "Other Worlds" sticker.

Each library system dreams up companion enticements. Arlington County, for example, takes advantage of their Apple IIe to print T-shirt logos. Montgomery County hires clowns and magicians to make the rounds of libraries, and Prince George's County branches hook up with local nature centers to bring animals to the library.

Quay talks about ways to use these programs to

extend summer reading. "We'll set out a number of books that are related to the program—something on squirmy things in the Chesapeake Bay, for instance—and point them out to the children. And if they take them home and look at them, they can come back and earn a sticker."

Children who fill in all the stickers normally earn some sort of goodie at the end of the program, anything from having their name on the bulletin board to a celebration with cookies and movies.

But the real prize, says D.C.'s Salvadore, is keeping up reading skills. Stanford University did a study in 1983, she says, "showing that students who read for pleasure in the summer—even a little—retained or, in some cases, gained skills." Children who throw down all books outside of school tend to lose hard-won skills.

Moreover, child psychologists and educators have pointed out the importance of reading for pleasure, says Salvadore. "We tend to bore children to death in school," she says, "but if we allow them to read for pleasure, we pique their interest in reading for a lifetime."

For both lifetime and summer readers, there's something really special about owning a book. And quite a few places offer a chance to do just that without a serious drain on the pocketbook.

AKJ Warehouse in Rockville, a paperback wholesaler that feeds elementary and intermediate school book fairs in this area and Reading Is Fundamental programs across the country, has its annual blow-out, half-price, get-em-by-the-dozen book sale in early June.

"We sell authors like Beverly Cleary, Judy Blume, and E.B. White, plus a whole slew of classics, biographies, histories, dictionaries, Easy to Read books, Choose Your Own Adventure books," says a spokesman. Prices are normally low; really low.

Discounts are also available all summer at Bradlee's, which has worked with the Greater Washington Reading Council to pinpoint appropriate books for young readers. "They helped us come up with a list of about 50 titles, some of which we don't normally carry, people such as (poet) Shel Silverstein and the Berenstain Bears," says spokeswoman Sharon Carter.

Reading Council member Betty Ann Armstrong also helped produce a brochure the store offers free to customers. It gives guidelines for reading aloud with children and includes the list of recommended books, broken down by appropriate age group. All these books will be discounted 20 percent during the summer. In addition, every week the store takes an extra 10 percent off two books.

Between the stores and the libraries, your child should be able to find something to read beside the pool, on the way to the roller coaster, or by the glare of MTV.

Getting into Reading
Library Programs
- *Libraries on Andrews and Bolling Air Force*

Bases and in Montgomery, Prince George's, Prince William, Arlington and Fairfax Counties, as well as Alexandria, Falls Church and the District, hold summer reading programs. They're aimed at, but not limited to, ages 6 to 12. Children sign up at their local library and receive stickers for eight different categories of books. Films, storytelling, mime, puppets, computers, and nature programs available in different libraries. For more information phone the library nearest you.

Children's Bookstores

- *A Happy Thought, 4836 MacArthur Boulevard N.W., Washington.*
- *A Likely Story, 110 South West Street, Alexandria, Virginia.*
- *Barcroft Books, 6349 Columbia Pike, Bailey's Crossroads, Virginia.*
- *Books Unlimited, 2729 Wilson Boulevard, Arlington, Virginia.*
- *Bookstall, 9927 Falls Road, Potomac, Maryland.*
- *Cheshire Cat, 5512 Connecticut Avenue N.W., Washington.*
- *Cover to Cover Jr. Editions, 2049 Columbia Mall, Columbia, Maryland.*
- *Cricket Bookshop, 17800 New Hampshire Avenue, Ashton, Maryland.*
- *Fairy Godmother, 319 7th Street, S.E., Washington.*
- *Lowen's, 7201 Wisconsin Avenue, Bethesda, Maryland.*
- *Storybook Palace, 9538 Old Keene Mill Road,*

Burke, Virginia.
• Special Events
• *AKJ Warehouse Sale. Annual, one-week warehouse sale held in June (see above for details) 12128 Nebel Street, Rockville, Maryland, 770-4030.*

SATURDAY MUSIC LESSONS FOR A SONG

Every Saturday morning, Coolidge High School in northwest Washington comes alive with the sound of music.

In the auditorium, conductor Lyn McLain is pulling the strings of the D.C. Youth Orchestra – the most senior of the four orchestras that operate under the DCYO Program – through a Brandenburg Concerto.

In the gym, the elementary orchestra is tuning up, while around and about the three floors of classrooms, beginners are making their violins, violas, flutes, oboes, clarinets, bassoons, saxophones, trumpets, French horns, trombones, and cellos sing such tunes as "Mississippi Hot Dog" and "Long, Long Ago."

"I used to play cello bass," chimes in 6-year-old Ellen, hurrying along to her class, "but my Daddy says you can carry the violin more places."

Some 1,700 students from ages 5 to 10 receive free instruction in the instrument of their choice through the youth orchestra program. If they don't have their own instruments, most students can rent them from the orchestra for $50 per year.

The orchestra, founded in 1960 and open to all young people in the metropolitan area, has produced musicians who now play with the National Symphony, the New York Philharmonic, the Boston Symphony, and other orchestras.

"We're a program that offers an opportunity to learn to play and to perform in an ensemble," says founder and director McLain, a former music teacher at Coolidge High. "Performance is the key; performance is the place where they get to show what they've done."

Even the beginners perform regularly, in concerts for fellow students and families.

"One more time from the top," says trumpet instructor Cathy Fronck, prepping her class for a concert. "That was better—much better—than yesterday."

"Okay, you're making progress," says oboe teacher Lesley Nowell in a classroom down the locker-lined hall. "You have to play at least two notes before you take a breath. That keeps the notes connected so it doesn't sound so choppy. Let's play four measures and see if we can keep the notes together."

"One, two, ready, go!" says instructor Ron Aufmann, snapping his fingers to urge on his beginning clarinet students. "Good, people. Are we ready to speed it up yet? No? Okay, we'll play it anyway."

"Ready, violins? Let's see some good playing positions. Let it ring! (a ring means let it sound)," says teacher Kris Kuny, as his class rings out a rousing rendition of "Mississippi Hot Dog."

"Perfect!" trumpets teacher Terry Alvey to his novice trumpeteers. "See, you can do it...Now a little faster. Yeah, that's great! If you mess up, keep going. I'm going to play it with you."

In still another classroom, 8-year-old Chris is trying out a brand new bassoon.

"He just got this today," explains instructor Nicholas Wilkinson. "He's just big enough to handle it. Chris, you have to lift this finger up all the way. Let me see that thumb move."

As concert hour approaches, eager and nervous young musicians stream down the stairs and through the halls to the gym, where parents and students not performing that day are assembled on bleachers. The sound of the performers tuning up mixes with the noise of babies crying. Siblings squirm, but parents are all ears and very proud.

"This is wonderful," says one parent, watching her son raise the bow to his violin. "What's fun about music is making it with other people."

Tuning in to the Orchestra
• Young people between the ages of 5 and 19 residing anywhere in the metropolitan area are eligible to join the D.C. Youth Orchestra Program. For information on how to register or for the schedule of concerts, call 723-1612.

FOOD SCENE

On one side of the room hang a half dozen beef carcasses next to an undefeatably cheerful Sam Gadell. On the other are three little kids, fingers pinching their noses, refusing to budge. The room is cold and full of the odor of dead cow.

"You don't want to come over here?" he asks, puzzled. Three little heads shake. "Well, then, this is where we hang our beef, so it can air and get good and moldy and taste real good," he says, undaunted, continuing a patter that started when we walked into his meatlocker, Gadell's Gourmet Meats and Caterers, now in Chantilly, Virginia.

"And there's where we put the fat and bones we cut from the meat. Some people come to pick those up each week, and they use them to make fertilizer, perfume..."

"Perfume!" exclaims Megan, 9. "Out of that?"

She's noticed the odor, a smell that Gadell and his relatives in this family-owned business are apparently immune to. The meatlocker business is not pretty, a fact our cheerful guide compares with "anything you do that's really fun—when you make brownies, or do finger painting, you get really messy. But it makes something really good, right?" Well, yes, but..."And this makes our meat taste really good—not like at the grocery store, where everything comes in boxes," he believes.

We checked this out the next week at Giant Food, where groups of ten of more young children may tour their local store with the manager.

John Smith at the Yorketowne Giant in Fairfax told us they get most of their meat in boxes, "but we hang it for an hour or so to get rid of that boxed taste."

The room where meat is cut was off-limits to our tour "because the floor tends to be slippery," he explained, but most Giants have a see-through window separating the customer from the meat cutters, and the children can watch through there.

Instead of taking the kids behind the scenes, the tour concentrated on pointing out those things any customer can see if he looks. Like the nozzles that stick up inconspicuously in the produce section, where employees attach hoses for spraying the vegetables "to keep them crisp," he explains.

Or the unit pricing codes, which the manager used to show how incredibly expensive a six-pack of juice was compared to a large can. Our group, for whom large numbers are still somewhat of a mystery, scurried around the juice aisle trying to find the cheapest drink and finally settled on a large can of grapefruit juice. "But I don't like grapefruit juice," pointed out Giorgos, 6.

They did like the peanut butter from the peanut butter machine (which the attendant kindly took apart for the children to see) and the doughnuts from the bakery and were intrigued by the laser-powered scanner at the register. "Some of our tours spend a long time at the register—kids today in fourth or sixth grades know all about computers, and ask lots of questions," Smith reports.

Kids in the seventh grade and older are intrigued by the megacomputer out at Safeway's robot-operated warehouse in Landover, says its superintendant, Dave Frye. "They want to know how it operates, how it's programmed, how much those people get paid," he said, pointing to a young woman in her twenties who was managing the robot-operated end of the warehouse.

Here, the computer—which does everything from make appointments for the truck drivers who ring in the 1.5 million nonperishable items ("that way, we can get them in and out in a half-hour") and assign numbers to each box ("these tell the fork-lift operator where they go"), to dispatching the robots (or "robos", as they call them) to pick up boxes slated for longer-term storage on 90-foot-high, two-box-deep shelves.

The robos, which look like tiny flatcars, are guided along the floor by electrical impulses and pick up loads carefully evened and stacked for them by machine. These they carry to the high shelves, where they are lifted by a kind of elevator with arms and deposited in slots the computer knows are empty. Sometimes, to retrieve just the right package, the armed elevator has to move boxes around—a process Frye refers to as a "shuffle."

The computer that sorts all this out sits in an air-conditioned room in the middle of the 400,000 square foot warehouse, right next to the computer running the rest of the area. "Sometimes they talk to each other," Frye confides.

Watching the robos is the highlight of the tour and lately has become the ending point. But the kids who come to visit, though intrigued with the squat automatons, are more interested in the "variety of jobs available in the grocery business," says Frye. "Most people think of grocers as the lady who runs the cash register or the produce man," he explains. "Here, they see the forklift operators, truck drivers, computer programmers, accountants, all making enough money to support a family."

Watching these people in action makes a

significantly different outing in a museum-saturated town and seems to appeal to kids, perhaps because it explains one of the nittiest gritties of daily life: Food.

Megan summed it up best after the meatlocker tour: "It was gross, but interesting. I always wondered about that stuff."

Food Tours
• Gadell's Gourmet Meats and Caterers, 14303 Sullyfield Circle, Chantilly, Virginia. Tours for kids and adults, singly or in groups, can be arranged by calling 631-7711. Bring a sweater; much of the tour is in the walk-in freezers.
• Giant Food Stores. Groups of ten of more elementary-school-age children and older are welcome. Call 341-4710 to arrange a tour of the closest Giant.
• Safeway Distribution Center, 1501 Cabin Branch Road, Landover, Maryland, phone 386-6570 for a tour of at least two and up to forty seventh-grade and older kids.

FEEDING TIME AT THE SHARK TANK

As he carefully injects each defrosted smelt with a vitamin solution, Michael Bailey reflects on how he got into his chosen profession.

"Once when I was snorkeling as a kid, I saw a shark swimming nearby," he recalls. "I just stood and watched. It was beautiful."

Today, Bailey is a grown-up marine biologist and director of the National Aquarium in the basement of the Commerce Department in downtown Washington. One of his duties is to feed the sharks. Sometimes they get squid, sometimes beef hearts, but they like smelt best.

"It's the same kind you buy in the grocery stores," says Bailey, disappearing into the narrow, winding passages behind the tanks. When he reaches the back of the shark tank, he takes a smelt from the bucket and holds it in the water with his bare hand.

"I'll feed them until they don't look hungry," he says, dropping the smelt. "I've only been bitten once, by a tiny shark I was trying to force feed. Sharks in a feeding frenzy will bite—I've even seen them devour their own intestines—but I don't think sharks are as mean as people think. They may take a test bite and they may bite to defend their territory. In the ocean we might not know where their territory is. If there's a dog in a yard that's not fenced in, we might not know where its territory is, but the dog does. If sharks wanted to eat people, a lot more people would be eaten."

The sharks circle the meal, snapping up morsels.

"They circle their food," explains Bailey, pulling another smelt out of the bucket. "They don't rely on vision until the very end. They have a lateral line system—they can feel vibrations. It's something like hearing in humans. They can also smell and sense electrical charges. If a shark swims over a flounder that's submerged in sand, it knows the flounder is there by its electrical charge."

After a leisurely half-hour meal, the sharks have eaten only about a quarter of a pound of smelt each, less than half their usual ration. Bailey attributes this to colder-than-usual water in the tanks, which means that the sharks' body temperatures and appetites are lower than usual. Their neighbors get a bonus in the form of leftovers.

"Hi, Spunky," says Bailey, throwing a smelt to a green sea turtle he describes as a neat guy.

"Almost everything here will eat smelt. We try to duplicate each animal's natural diet, but we can't always. The rock beauty, for instance, eats live sponges. They're not easy to come by or to keep."

By the time Bailey has made his rounds and reappeared on the public side of the shark tank, most of the crowd has dispersed. But some hardcore shark fans are still watching the animals swim around.

"Aren't they pretty?" asks Bailey. "One of my favorite things is to go diving with sharks. I carry a little wooden dowel with a nail head in it to push them away with. Any time you're in the ocean, you're an outsider in their domain."

Then Bailey excuses himself to go talk with a boy who wants to be a shark person when he grows up.

Watching the Sharks Eat

- *For a schedule of feeding times for the sharks and the piranhas, call 377-2825. The National Aquarium, the nation's oldest, is located in the basement of the Commerce Department at 14th Street between E and Constitution Avenues, N.W., Washington. It's open daily, and there's a small admission fee. In addition to the shark feedings, there is a self-guided tour of about a thousand specimens, a touch tank especially for kids, and films.*
- *There's a bigger, government-supported National Aquarium in Baltimore, at the Inner Harbor, where all fish, including sharks, are fed by divers right in the tanks. For information, call 301-576-3810.*

ROLLING ALONG AT THE RINKS

'We're so old-fashioned we still do the Hokey Pokey," says Dennis Brown, manager of the Rockville Wheel-a-While roller skating rink.

Visits to his and other rinks, in fact, felt like a quick dive into the 1950s: 8-year-old boys hold each other's hands during the couples only skates; fathers buffer tiny tots hovering close to the edge of the rink; teenage boys haul their kid sisters around; and 10-year-old girls form lines of fast-rolling giggles.

Some things have changed from the skating days of yore, of course. Madonna and Pink Floyd, rather than organ music, blare over the loudspeaker; the crystal balls of the 1970s disco skating era turn on the ceiling; video games beep and zap in the corner; and the skates themselves are high tech improvements over the ones of yesteryear. But the atmosphere reeks of that rarest of 1980s commodities, innocent fun.

"We don't allow smoking or drinking, and we cater to young children," says Jack Becker, president of the Wheel-a-While chain which has eight rinks in this area. "Of course, some of these kids can be tricky, especially the junior-high age. We don't have trouble with the high school kids." Wheel-a-While has at least one guard on each rink at all times, but their main job is to pick up fallen skaters, Becker says.

Some other rinks cater to a faster crowd, and have as many as ten guards who are occasionally called on to break up fights.

Whatever their styles, most rinks fill with different types at different times, catering to singles, say, on Friday night, and families on Saturday afternoon.

Parents are warned to check things out before dropping off their kids. "We like to see the parent come in with their kids," Becker says. "For one thing, their children are usually the better behaved ones. And for another, the parents usually wind up skating, too."

Most rinks try to draw parents in by scheduling

family skates, when the children typically skate for free. Then there are skate-ins at public recreation centers, which tend to fill with the after-school elementary-age crowd or young teens, recreation managers say.

In addition, some rinks have a special time set aside just for new skaters, when they can learn simply to balance on skates without a lot of pros whizzing by.

"We started our kids at about 17 months," Dennis Brown says of his three children, third-generation skaters who now help behind the snack bar, "and I know a lot of pros who started theirs sooner. As soon as they can walk, they can skate."

Sam Gilyad, who manages the "last of the dinosaurs," the Alexandria Roller Rink (scheduled for imminent demolition as this is written), says his staff will sometimes tighten up a couple of wheels on neophyte youngsters' skates so they don't roll so freely.

"That way they learn to pick up their feet and walk in them," he says.

Other rinks encourage the youngsters to practice on the carpeted area or stay in the center of the rink with a parent by their side. And many of the local rinks, including Wheel-a-While, offer inexpensive classes to help the beginner. But Becker wonders how necessary these are.

"These days, parents all think the only way their kids can learn is with lessons—swimming lessons, bike lessons, roller skating lessons. Most kids learn just by doing it," he thinks.

For those who want to go beyond learning the scissors or the backward skate, some rinks teach artistic skating in group and private lessons. Graduates of these classes often join a club, such as Wheel-a-While's National Capital Dance and Figure Skating Club, and work toward competing in local, regional and national championships.

"Roller skating's just like ice skating, except that it's more graceful," says Dennis Brown's father, Tom, who ran the Alexandria Roller Rink for 26 years. "All the stuff you see Peggy Fleming and Dorothy Hamill doing on ice, you can do on roller skates," he says. Brown and his wife used to dance routines, and he remembers the days when rinks were full of such couples. "It was like a show," he says.

More than the rinks have changed since then: for instance, the price of a pair of skates. Roller skates today can set you back anywhere from $40 to $400, covering a range in quality comparable to a Volkswagen to Cadillac spread, says Gilyad. His rink can rent you "something in a Buick."

"You can still buy $20 or $30 skates," says Becker, "but the boot is probably made of vinyl, which makes your foot sweat, and the wheels aren't that good."

Outstanding boots, Gilyad says, are double-lined with leather to give good support, and constructed so that "at the end of the evening, your foot doesn't ache."

With the way children's feet grow, Becker says, most parents would be better off simply renting skates. But committed skaters—like Dennis Brown's daughters, who practice their dance routines three hours a day—prefer to buy their own skates.

Such "artistic" or "freestyle" skating is on the way up, says Becker, whereas recreational skating is on the way down. "We die on weeknights," Dennis Brown acknowledges. "I think everyone's home with the VCR."

That can make skating on a week night more fun, say the skaters; you're less likely to encounter a crowd. Evenings are also more likely to be given over to fitness-conscious adults, enjoying the aerobic aspects of whirling around a rink.

But most rinks still see themselves, as Dennis Brown puts it, as "glorified babysitters. For the price of a movie," he points out, "your kid gets not 90 minutes of sitting but three hours of entertainment. And if you're lucky, they go home tired and ready for bed."

Many rinks cater to Scout groups, day care centers, handicapped schools, and birthday parties, offering package deals with party favors and a special room or table.

Whether you're coming for a party, a class, or just an afternoon out of the house, a roller rink can offer an easy escape.

Besides, it's the only place in the Washington metropolitan area where our 11-year-old daughter let us hold her hand in public.

Roll Out the Rinks
* *Skating is available at perhaps a dozen professional rinks and many recreation centers in the area. Here's a sampling.*

Virginia
* *Wheel-a-While, 577-8889, eight locations in the metropolitan area. Skating seven evenings per week plus weekend and school holiday matinees. Admission, plus skate rental fee. Group and private instruction; birthday party package; skating club; and private rental.*
* *Reston Skateway, 471-5008, 1800 Michael Faraday Court. Open seven evenings plus weekends and Monday matinees. Thursday is family night; games at all sessions. Admission plus skate rental fee. Lessons for beginners. Small rink, children not allowed to leave building without parents.*
* *Arlington County Community Centers, 558-2700. Skating every Saturday night at Thomas Jefferson Community Center; occasional Friday nights plus Wednesday after school at Madison Community Center; admission plus skate rental.*

Maryland
* *Wheel-a-While. See Virginia listing above.*
* *Montgomery County Recreation Department, 540-1300. Skating at three community centers in the northern part of the county—Longwood (Olney), Upper County (Gaithersburg), and Plumgar (Germantown), usually on Friday nights, for a small skate rental fee.*
* *Prince George's Park and Recreation*

Department—North, 445-4500; Central, 249-9220; South, 248-1260. Hours and sites vary widely in the three sections. For information, call the above number for your area, or your local community center. Admission, plus skate rental fee.
Washington
• *D.C. Recreation Department, 576-6874, free skating sessions at 29 centers during the winter months, typically during the week. Participants must bring their own skates. Call for dates and locations.*

LEARNING LABS AT THE ZOO

Dr. Dale Marcellini thinks he knows why the reptile and amphibian house ranks second in popularity only to the panda pad at the National Zoo.

"People either love them or think they're awful," says Marcellini, who's curator of the creepy-crawlies. "And do people like awful things? Of course! That's why they go to horror movies—to be titillated."

Whether you love reptiles or think they're awful, you can learn about them in Herplab, one of three learning laboratories for children and adults at the

zoo. Herplab, short for herpetology laboratory, features recordings of frog calls, films of lizard fights, tortoise skeletons to piece together, even a live snake-of-the-day and a frog-of-the-day you can check out and get to know.

As soon as one of these critters is checked out and taken in its own plastic box to one of the tables, the human question-asking reflex is activated.

"Why is it sticking out its tongue?" asks a visitor staring at a corn snake in a box with a mirror on the bottom that reflects the snake's corn-kernel-like underbelly.

The answer (the snake is not sticking its tongue out at you—it's using its tongue to taste and smell the air) is right there in the same box, separated from the snake by a partition. Visitors' questions are anticipated even before they're asked, thanks to a team of experts who spent three years setting up Herplab under a grant from the National Science Foundation.

"We sat down with families and found out what they wanted to know," says Judith White, the zoo's education chief. "Then we talked about what we thought was important. We tried out prototypes of the boxes on visitors to the zoo, then revised them. What we're doing is developing materials to help families learn biological principles, using reptiles as tools. Most reptiles are small, so they're easier to handle than mammals, and it's easier to look at many different species."

Perhaps White is partial to reptiles because she's married to Marcellini, whom she met when, as new employees of the zoo, they were being fingerprinted. The couple does not, however, keep any creepy-crawlies at home.

"Snakes in your house are like plants, not pets," says Marcellini. "As pets they're terribly boring. I used to have lizards. Lizards are somewhat more social, more complicated. They're the intellectuals of the reptile world."

Lizards' social (some might say antisocial) activity has inspired a movie shown at Herplab. Informally dubbed "Bonzo Meets Godzilla," the film illustrates the fact that lizards, like lions and bears, are territorial.

Filmed on location at Herplab, the short flick opens with a shot of a male kingfish lizard resting on a rock on its own turf. Enter a young upstart. The challenger flaps his dewlap (a reddish bag of skin between the jaws). In lizard terms, this is like waving a red flag. The challenge is met by the incumbent's dewlap, and the battle is joined.

To find out which of the leaping lizards win the turf battle, you'll have to see the movie—and play the territoriality board game and read the coordinating comic book. They're yours for the asking, at Herplab.

Labs and Special Events at the Zoo

• In addition to Herplab, the zoo houses Birdlab, in the Bird House, and Zoolab, in the Education Building. All are free and open various hours. Another special attraction is a popular series called "Sunday Afternoon at the Zoo." This winter

series might include a tour of the zoo kitchens, films, puppet shows, and craft activities. For information about all of the above, call 673-4717. National Zoological Park entrances are on Beach Drive, Adams Mill Road, and 3000 Connecticut Avenue N.W., Washington.

TRULY LITTLE THEATER

When director Mimi Turner of the Mt. Vernon Community Children's Theatre found her cast backstage at one point in their rigorous, four-day-per-week rehearsal schedule, they were "literally rolling around on the floor, biting each other's ankles," she says.

Ten minutes later they were up on the stage, mimicking the ennui-ridden young aristocrats in "The Importance of Being Earnest" and delivering Oscar Wilde's biting aphorisms with sophisticated timing.

Such are the extremes of children's theater, one of the livelier arts. Half a dozen children's troupes in this area take kids as young as six through the acting business, giving them what director Lenore Riegal of the Trinity Players Children's Theater calls "real-life skills. It helps in meeting people, talking with people, talking before a group," she thinks.

"I guess it's helped with oral reports and stuff like that," muses 14-year-old Julia of the Mt. Vernon troupe, but she sees a much more practical side: "I just moved here two months ago, and I came to this play and made all these friends," she says brightly.

There may even be monetary value to this lively art. Trinity Players graduates have starred in the Ford's Theater production of "A Christmas Carol" and the NBC series "Our House;" other troupes have had members in local theater and TV casts.

But to be members, they first have to get past the auditions—experiences that three-time-star Alice, a 12-year-old with the Children's Theatre of Arlington, says can be "pretty disappointing."

"It's a hard way to learn that life is unfair," says CTA's Marcy Ubois. "We try to relax the kids and make it fun." In addition to having the children read lines from the play, the Arlington group usually calls for "some sort of improvisation, sometimes some mime," she says.

"They usually ask us to be animals," says 12-year-old Sean, who's been in six productions. "Once they told us to be lumps of clay turning into something."

Watching other kids cope with these orders "gives you ideas and sometimes you can do better," says Hogan. "But at least you've learned something," she believes.

The directors, in turn, watch the children, looking for certain heights and types, voices that project and "good behavior," says Ubois. "So if you don't make it," says young star Hogan, "it's probably because you don't fit the type, not because you can't act."

Once chosen, the group settles into six- to eight-week rehearsal schedules that require a "real commitment," says director Ubois. Fourteen-year-old Judd, who played Earnest in the Mt. Vernon production, confesses that homework sometimes suffers: "You go to school, you go to rehearsal, you go home and eat dinner, you do your homework, you go to bed," is how he describes the rehearsal day, saying that when the play ends, he's planning on some "lazy days at home."

Children with lazy days available sometimes do better than the busy soccer, French, and gymnastics stars of school, says Trinity's director Riegal. "You'd be surprised at how ordinary these kids are. Then they get up on the stage, and something magic happens," she says.

The children involved are much more specific on what kinds of kids do best: "Someone who's spazzy, but not overly spazzy," explains Hogan—using a phrase that apparently means someone who is enthusiastic, but not silly.

"Someone who's not a nerd," states Sean, who adds that "it can be pretty rough backstage," if you don't fit in. "I've come down on people who were too weird," he says.

But for the Mt. Vernon group, the enemy is somewhat larger. "Parents!" they answer in chorus, when asked for the worst part of children's theater. "They keep telling us we're almost adults, and expect us to behave like adults," says Judd, who admits that the troupe often got "pretty obnoxious" during rehearsals. But "this is the Mt. Vernon Children's Theatre, get it? It's supposed to be for children."

High expectations are common among the adult supporters of these groups, typically parents who have been roped in to do makeup and costumes and sell tickets. The Arlington group gets its costume and set designers from Arlington County government; the rest struggle along on ticket sales and community support. Some, like the Bethesda Academy for the Performing Arts, charge their troupers a fee "to cover costumes and scenery," says a spokesman.

All these groups tend to produce what Judd calls "kiddie shows—Winnie the Pooh, stuff like that," which appeal to audiences composed of the actors' friends and relatives. But while the quality of a few productions can best be described as "cute," directors strive toward something bordering on legitimate.

"We try to be professional, to give the children an experience in professional theater," says Arlington's Ubois, although her cast goes out to the lobby after a show to sign autographs, something legitimate theater would never allow. "But they love it," she justifies. "That's their reward."

"I like it when you get up on stage and make a fool of yourself and the audience laughs with you," says 12-year-old Stephen, Algernon in the Mt. Vernon production. "That's what's fun."

In children's theater, like its parent, they do it for the applause.

Getting into Children's Theater
Washington
- *Trinity Players Children's Theater, Georgetown, 965-4680. Two to three productions per year.*
- *Capitol Hill Arts Workshop, 547-6839. Puts on a fundraiser show with child actors.*

Maryland
- *Adventure Theatre, Glen Echo, 320-5331. A wide variety of classes for ages 5 and up, some leading to performance. Fee.*
- *Bethesda Academy of the Performing Arts, Bethesda, 320-2550. Classes in various theater arts; children auditioned from classes into four different troupes. Fee.*
- *Jewish Community Center, Rockville, 881-0100, ext. 340. Children's classes in creative drama for first grade through teens.*
- *Montgomery County Recreation Department, Wheaton, 468-4172. Children's theater classes plus day and resident camps, and performance labs.*

Virginia
- *Children's Theatre of Arlington, 739-2903. Three major productions per year, plus classes and summer camp. Fees for classes and camp only.*
- *Fairfax County Children's Theater, 691-2671. Three productions, plus summer activites.*
- *Mt. Vernon Community Children's Theatre, 768-7689. Three productions, plus classes.*

SEEING HOW OTHERS SEE

There are many paths to God, and in a country as religiously diverse as this one, it behooves us to help our children appreciate the sincerity of those on paths we've not taken.

Most of us bump up against others' religions throughout life—as we're invited to friends' weddings, baptisms, and children's christenings, or (if we're lucky) asked to participate in others' Passover meals or Christmas dinners.

Orchestrating such user-friendly religious experiences for your children may be a little difficult. You might want to consider complementing them with visits to the numerous orthodox church festivals around, Christian Science lectures, or any one of the scores of local churches, synagogues, mosques, and temples in the Washington area.

We've scouted out a quartet that will show your children four very different paths to the same God. We advise that you skip services—how would you feel if others came to observe you worshipping? Also, give the kids some idea of what they're about to see, and teach them the first step to worshipping—reverential quiet, or at least quiet—while you're there. Here they are:

American Fazl Mosque—2141 Leroy Place N.W., Washington, 232-3737. Open "morning to evening," says a spokesman, with services at 1:30, 3:30, 5 and

7. The main features are a minaret where the congregation is called to worship, a pool for ritual ablutions, and a rug-filled interior where worshippers kneel and pray, facing Mecca (see the niche in the wall to find which direction to face), or listen to a Friday sermon from the khatib (preacher) standing at the top of those ornate stairs (minbar). You must take off your shoes to enter the mosque; when we were there, a guide asked me to cover my hair. The Moslems are linked to Jews and Christians through Abraham who, with Hagar, fathered Ishmael (see Genesis 16); you can tell your children that the God they worship in this light, beautiful room is the God of Abraham.

B'nai B'rith Klutznick Museum—1640 Rhode Island Avenue N.W., Washington, 857-6583. Open Sunday—Friday from 10 to 5; closed Saturdays, legal holidays, and Jewish holidays. This is a small and approachable museum that details Jewish daily life and the calendar of celebrations, providing simple explanations and artifacts for each. The day we were there, they showed a cartoon about Hanukah that helped our non-Jewish children understand the holidays; so did the inexpensive dreidels we bought at the gift shop. The museum artifacts—hand-embroidered Torah coverings, seder plates, and those noisemakers they use in Purim—were fun to ogle. The whole thing took perhaps a half-hour, and the kids came away with a strong sense of the Jewish religion as our heritage.

Franciscan Monastery—1400 Quincy Street N.E.,

Washington, 526-6800. Tours daily on the hour from 9 to 4, except lunch hour. This is a fun trip with kids; the monastery contains reproductions of the early Christian catacombs, life-sized models of the birth and crucifixion of Jesus, a portico with the Lord's Prayer translated into dozens of languages, and beautiful grounds containing duplicates of religious sites like the Grotto at Lourdes. The whole tour is a good synopsis of the significant events in mainline Christianity.

Mormon Temple—The Washington Temple of the Church of Jesus Christ of the Latter-Day Saints, 9900 Stoneybrook Drive, Kensington, Maryland, 526-6800. Open daily from 10 to 9:30. This is that magnificent, fairy-castle-looking thing you see along the Beltway, with the angel Moroni, an ancient American prophet in the Mormon religion, blowing his trumpet to the sky. The temple—open only to members of the church—is used chiefly for weddings, meetings, and "ancestral baptisms." It's a huge (160,000-square foot) marble structure with translucent marble and fractured-glass windows, topped by six gold-covered spires and the 2½ ton Moroni figure. Open to the public is the visitors center next door, where you can see films describing the temple, the religion, and various holidays, plus dioramas showing the founding and struggles of the Mormon people. At least some of this will be familiar to mainline Christians (the Mormon religion centers on Jesus Christ); those who believe in an afterlife may be intrigued by their vision, where families are "sealed" in eternity. One warning: Guides sometimes take your visit as evidence that you're interested in their religion; one followed us out to the parking lot with a Book of Mormon.

SUNNY DAYS

FINDING THE SUMMER CAMPS

When the icicles mount under the eaves and the kids spend their weekends avoiding homework and putting off their science fair project, it's time to get your life in order.

We're talking about summer here. Late winter is time, we fear, to get your plans shaped up and your down payments in for camp—or backpacking, or trekking through Europe, or whatever your kids plan to do once school ends.

For one thing, it may take you until the middle of June to look into catalogs, send off for brochures and interview the kid down the street who took that neat horseback/camping trip in Colorado last year.

But in late winter and early spring, we can get you dozens of camp directors under one roof and a staff of people who are experts at arranging fascinating, mind-expanding summer experiences for the under-20 set.

Camp advisers in the area range from freelancers like Elizabeth Sibbett, who knows the local overnight camps like probably no one else, to organizations like the American Camping Association and Tips on Trips and Camps, started in 1971 by mothers looking for alternatives to the usual camping scene for their children.

The latter two put on camp fairs that are free for all participants. But if a camper signs up, the camp pays Tips a small percentage fee—a fee which, detractors say, makes them brokers for only the wealthiest clients and toniest camps. Tips earns this fee by setting up dozens of these meetings around the country, and sending inspectors to the camps "at least once every three years," says their spokesman, Nancy Ludwig. "We only pick programs we'd feel comfortable sending our own children to," she adds.

At a meeting we witnessed, Tips personnel greeted parents and campers at the door and had them fill out forms to determine their interests.

Then the Tips people went to work trying to match the child with a handful of possible camp experiences—anything from biking for a month, learning French on the Riviera, touring college campuses in the Northeast and backpacking in Colorado.

The Tips people trot campers and their parents around to meet camp directors, and also hand them brochures and applications from other camps whose directors aren't present.

Here's how it might work for you: Say your 15-year-old is a third-year French student who loves the language. The Tips people will probably point out the language immersion programs, like the International Cultural Institute.

That's a fairly new outfit which drills students in the finer points of conversational French while putting them up in a chateau in the south of

France for 12 days. There, they "adjust to the culture," says a spokesman, "and learn to do little things, like make a phone call."

Then each child goes solo into a French home for three weeks, where there's "a child of the same age in the family who wants to have an American come and stay," says the spokesman. It's cultural immersion on a natural level, "and their French really improves," she says.

Maybe it's not French you want to improve, but tennis, or scuba diving. Or perhaps your child wants to take this summer to master the computer or ballet. Camps to develop all these skills exist, and many send their directors and slide shows to these meetings.

There you'll have a chance, as Bill Cole from the American Camping Association puts it, to "meet with the directors, and see if you're comfortable with them and the amount of structure they offer. Is this the kind of person you want to be responsible for your child this summer?" he asks.

The American Camping Association, which has been accreditating camps for the last 75 years, usually holds two large camp fairs in early Spring with representatives from a much broader range of camping experiences. "There's a camp here to fit every pocketbook," he says, "including some day camps from the Washington area."

But at Tips on Trips and Camps, although they represent a number of traditional activities for all ages, the emphasis seems to be on razzle-dazzle adventures for the teenager—particularly the teen from the two-income family.

"There used to be just these broad interest camps where you went as a kid and came back as a teenager to be a counselor," says Tips' Ludwig.

But with vast increases in the number of two-income families and single parents, it's becoming obvious that "keeping a teenager occupied during the day is very important," says Ludwig.

So they've gathered directors from places like Longacre Farm, a working farm in Pennsylvania where kids learn to cook for a crowd, birth pigs, and build hen houses—or from Trailmarks, a camping trip that stays in college dorms, giving teens a chance to tour the campuses.

Then there are backpacking or biking tours of New England, the West, or several countries in Europe, designed for a teen who "probably doesn't enjoy traveling with his parents, but could get a lot out of a trip with other teens," says ACA's Cole.

Picking and choosing among these various adventures is a matter of mixing available monies with the child's interests, degree of commitment, and need for structure.

"If you're a fairly low-key, loose kind of family," says Cole, "your child might feel uncomfortable in a highly structured program, and vice versa."

Similarly, if your motive for sending the child to camp doesn't match the goals of the camp, you may be setting him up for a bad time. "We're not a babysitting service," says one camp director. "If you just want to get rid of your kids for the summer, don't send them here."

If you want your child to learn French, but she just wants to play tennis, it probably will waste your money to enroll her in a language immersion program, for instance.

The Tips people, as well as those running the ACA Camp Fair in March, should be able to steer you around most of these obstacles. But the final criterion for a good camping experience, say the experts, should come from the camper himself—enthusiasm.

And bringing your camper to the fair, where he can see the slides and ask the questions, should either generate that needed excitement or show you clearly that something that looks good on paper falls flat face to face. Chances are, though, that the key for turning your child on lies somewhere in those two-dozen-plus choices.

Then he can get back to avoiding his homework and putting off his science fair project.

Finding the Camps
- *American Camping Association, 362-4360.*
- *Camp Advisory Service, Elizabeth Sibbett, 493-8474.*
- *Tips and Trips on Camps, 530-3313.*

AMBUSHING YOUR OWN GREAT PUMPKIN

"**H**ere it comes!" yells 9-year-old Katie as a tractor-pulled haywagon lumbers down the hill and parks near the stand at Potomac Vegetable Farms, a bucolic family farm in the shadow of Tysons Corner. This is the vehicle that will transport us—four adults, six children, and one Cabbage Patch Kid—to the farm's far-flung pumpkin patch.

There are quicker and easier ways to buy a pumpkin. The supermarkets are full of them, and supermarket prices are competitive with pick-your-own prices. But when you pick your own pumpkins, you get a bonus: a fall adventure in the country.

At Potomac Vegetable Farms, the haywagon shuttle leaves for the pumpkin patch several times

each weekend afternoon. At other times you're welcome to hike it, but if you pick a weighty pumpkin, it's a heavy walk back.

"Want to see the tractor, Michael?" prompts a father who wants to see the tractor while the other children scramble aboard, roll in the hay, throw it at each other and dive into it, yelling, "GI Joe, American Hero!"

The hay, confesses our genial driver, is really straw and its main function seems to be to cushion the shock as we bounce up the hill past the raspberry patch, the cider shed, and the goose pen and cross a field where a cow grazes among rusted farm implements. Then we lurch downhill, into fall-smelling woods.

"We're following the trail of pumpkins," exclaims my 3-year-old, noting the pumpkins sitting on up-ended baskets on either side of the dirt path. The trail ends at the pumpkin patch, where bright orange pumpkins peek from under green leaves.

"The pumpkins got ripe early this year and the weeds just grew up over them," explains our driver, as the kids jump out of the wagon in search of perfect potential jack-o-lanterns. Perfection, however, is in the eye of the beholder.

"Here's one with a scar," says 4-year-old Andrew, gleefully lugging an oversized pumpkin with a lurid brown gash down the middle of what would be its face. "I'm going to call him Scarface."

At Butler's Orchard in Germantown, some pumpkins are already in Halloween dress.

"Mom, I just saw a man with a pumpkin head,"

says my 3-year-old. "And that one's a lady, it has make-up on. And Mickey Mouse is in the train. And there's a witch and a house and a horsey!"

Pumpkins growing quietly in a field don't generate this kind of excitement, and Butler's has artfully created "Pumpkinland," a sort of storyland between the pumpkin patch and picnic area. The pumpkins, fleshed out with large zucchini limbs, perform in tableaux. A pumpkin version of Lucy dispenses psychiatric advice while a pumpkin Snoopy lounges on his doghouse, and a pumpkin Charlie Brown looks suitably downcast. A pumpkin-faced pirate opens an old chest filled with a treasure of golden gourds. The big, bad wolf, menacing in spite of his pumpkin face, preys on three pumpkin pigs. There are also the Old Woman in the Shoe, Spiderman, and a cast of hundreds.

For the raw material to create your own Snoopy or Spiderman, you have to go to the pumpkin patch, where pumpkins and gourds grow among the cornstalks.

"This one's a girl because it has curls," says a little girl, choosing a pumpkin with some sort of growth on both sides.

For a small boy, the choice is dictated by practical considerations.

"This is the only one he can carry, so it's going to be his," says his mother.

At Robin Hill Farm Nursery, a 152 acre spread in rural Prince George's County, there's a big bright orange fiberglass pumpkin shell to play in, but the main attractions are the live animals.

"Hi, piggy. Hi, pig pig," says my 3-year-old, running from the baby pigs to the rabbits to the ducks to the calf. For pumpkin-picking season, farmers have taken the animals out of the fields, ponds, and barns and placed them in pens where visiting children can see and pet them. There are also picnic tables on the grounds and, on weekend afternoons, hayrides around the farm.

The pumpkins are strewn in a field that stretches as far as the eye can see. After toying with a bulbous green-and-orange number, my daughter chose a conventional orange pumpkin, medium size.

"It's not a daddy pumpkin. It's not a mommy one. It's not a baby one," she explains. "It's a sister pumpkin."

Pumpkin Picking Places
* *The following farms usually feature pick-your-own pumpkins in the weeks preceding Halloween. Call for details and directions.*
* *In Virginia: Potomac Vegetable Farms, Vienna, 703-759-2119.*
* *In Maryland: Butler's Orchard, Germantown, 301-972-3299; Robin Hill Farm Nursery, Brandywine, 301-579-6844; Pumphrey's Home Grown, Millersville, 301-987-0669; Becraft's Farm Produce, Silver Spring, 301-236-4545; Homestead Farm, Poolesville, 301-428-3454; Rock Hill Orchard, Mt. Airy, 301-831-7427; Darrow Berry Farm, Glenn Dale, 301-390-6611, E.A. Parker and Sons, Clinton, 301-292-3940.*

THE HORSES OF FORT MYER

The cavalry no longer charges up the hill in battle, but there are still some horses on active duty in the US Army. They keep the caissons rolling along at military funerals and other ceremonies, and they receive visitors every day from noon to 4 p.m. at the Fort Myer stables in Virginia.

"This is Jimmy C., named after President Carter," said a soldier, leading one adult and three child visitors through the stables. Jimmy C., a mixed Appaloosa, is one of a group of about 15 white horses that form one team at Fort Myer. There is an equal number of black horses, and the two teams divide up the military funerals, two or three of which occur every day.

White-horse tack (saddles and stuff) and black-horse tack are kept in separate tack rooms, even though all the gear looks exactly the same.

"It's all spit-shined every day," said our guide, one of the soldiers who groom and exercise the horses and ride in the funerals. The stable is hosed down every day and the horses are groomed every day. Before every ceremonial outing, the horses are led through a door marked "watch room" for a good scrub. They are so clean the stable doesn't smell like a stable.

"This is Harvey," said our guide, opening the door of the stall of one of the white horses and introducing him to the children. "He's one of the gentlest horses I know with children."

After Harvey had good-naturedly endured petting by three pairs of hands, we moved on to see the wagons. There's the Tally Ho Wagon, a vintage coach of English origin that carries retirees around to review the troops at military retirement ceremonies, and the Marriage Carriage, a nineteenth century brougham used to carry military brides and grooms from the chapel to the wedding reception.

"A lot of these things were given to us by the Smithsonian Institution because they knew we had a use for them," explained the guide.

Not so the flat black wagon that has a room practically to itself. "That's the caisson that was used to carry Kennedy," he explained. Caissons, he added, were originally used to pull cannons around battlefields. When cannons became obsolete, the caissons were converted to pulling caskets. Six horses pull each caisson.

"This is a dummy casket, used for cremations," said the guide, pointing to an oak box with a barely perceptible trap door. The casket is placed on the caisson with the urn of ashes inside, but when it's time for burial the urn is removed and buried without the casket.

"This is a military tradition that goes back to the days of Ghenghis Khan," continued the guide, leading his charges to a display of caparisoned tack. "Cap" tack, used at funerals of high-ranking officers and presidents, consists of the officer's saber and his boots, turned backwards in the stirrups. In Ghenghis Khan's day the horse got buried with its master to serve him in the afterlife. But at Arlington Cemetery, the tradition stops at the grave site. The caparisoned riderless horse who marched in President Kennedy's funeral, Black Jack, attracted a coterie of admirers, one of whom used to bake him an oatcake on every birthday. Black Jack has since died, but others carry on the tradition.

Most of the black horses were out working a funeral the day of our visit, but a few remained in the barn. Some were being exercised in an outdoor ring next to the stable and some were just resting in their stalls.

"That's a Morgan, our only registered horse," continued the guide. "And this one's part Clydesdale. He weighs 1,800 pounds. And this is Oklahoma, the only horse I know who gives kisses."

The guide opened the door of the stall. Three little girls waited with upturned faces, but Oklahoma apparently wasn't in the mood.

Visiting the Horses
• *The stables are open daily from noon to 4 p.m. on the grounds of Fort Myer in Arlington. Ask the guard at the gate for directions to the stables. Telephone: 696-3568.*

GROUNDS FOR PLAY

Tried any good playgrounds lately? The woods are literally full of them in this area. They feature everything from massive multi-tiered wooden structures dripping with slides, tires, swings, ropes, and tunnels, to imaginative duplicates of Cinderella's carriage, fire engines, swimming dolphins, and Pac-Man computer mazes.

We asked local park and recreation authorities for the names of unusual sites, those loaded up with equipment or featuring truly unique designs. What we found, circling the Beltway, was a kind of minihistory of the last 25 years, done in playgrounds. Starting with the 1960s-type brightly painted metal of places like Wheaton Regional Park, playground equipment has grown to include wood, rubber, and plastic, while the ground covers went from sand to wood chips to gravelly pebbles.

The latest word in this area comes from designers like Robert Leathers. He's an Ithaca, New York-based consultant who works with schools, churches, synagogues, and other groups to develop their playground, turning the whole process into an educational, community-directed show.

First, he visits with the children most likely to use the playground, asking for their ideas and sketching while they speak. The kids are already primed by their teachers, who get them to write essays and draw pictures of their ideal playground first, and Leathers is apparently quite good about weeding out the impossible, like saunas, while including the unlikely, like computer-type mazes.

Then the group goes looking for money, equipment, supplies, and volunteers, bringing in as many community members as possible "so they'll have a stake in it," says Barbara Effrom, general coordinator of the playground group at Abingdon School in Arlington, who worked with Leathers in 1984. "He thinks you prevent vandalism if those most likely to commit it had a hand in building the place," she says.

All this effort culminates in a four-day construction blitz, producing large, interconnected

wooden structures. Leathers likes to work in materials like conveyer belts, rubber-coated steel cables, oversized tires, and discarded steering wheels, making playgrounds that are abstract enough to fit many different imaginations.

They're also physically challenging, like all good playground equipment. Throughout the area we found pieces that help children both develop their muscles and become more aware of their bodies— giant teeter-totters, slides made of rollers, swings, and spring-mounted riding toys.

Designers are also obviously bearing safety in mind, you see very few tall slides or high, unenclosed swings anymore. But those who supervise playgrounds caution that even superbly designed equipment can be the source of accidents among those of admittedly underdeveloped, immature judgment. So watch 'em.

Here, then, is a list of some of the best.

Virginia
• *Abingdon Elementary School, 3035 South Abingdon Street, 845-7664. One of the largest Robert Leathers designs in the area, the playground arose from a $35,000 budget and the work of 1,100 volunteers. It's designed in the shape of the United States (the high climbers are the Rockies, the alligator is Florida) and includes areas accessible to the school's one handicapped class. To get there, take I-395 South to Route 7 West. From Route 7, take a right onto South 28th Street; this becomes South 29th. Wind through the condominiums past*

two main roads to the school, which is behind some tennis courts. The playground is behind the school.

• *Haycock Elementary School, 6616 Haycock Road, Falls Church, 532-4340. This four-year-old Robert Leathers design includes a Pac Man-type computer maze, four slides (one of them circular), a "rocket ship," numerous large tire swings and tire tunnels, and an amphitheater where the local teens like to try out their break-dancing skills. To get there, take I-66 West to the Sycamore Street exit. Go right towards Arlington, and make a left at Washington Boulevard. Follow Washington Boulevard straight, past the entrance to I-66, until it curves around to your right and becomes Westmoreland Road. Take Westmoreland to Haycock, make a left; school is on your immediate right.*

• *Oakwood School, 7210 Braddock Road, Annandale, 941-5788. Robert Leathers designed this in conjunction with the school's specialized staff to meet the needs of children with gross motor dysfunctions. The wooden structure, taken as a whole, is a course to develop big muscle skills. To get there, take I-395 to 236 West; go on 236 to Braddock Road (near the Bradlee's) and make a left onto Braddock Road. The school is a few miles down, one block past the intersection with Backlick Road, on the right.*

• *Tuckahoe Park, Lee Highway and Sycamore Streets, Arlington. A very early version of the "log city" type playground, Tuckahoe was designed 16 years ago by two local landscape architects. It includes a massive concrete, rock-studded mountain pierced by a tunnel and attached to a high wooden climbing structure. There are two very long slides and a set of high swings. NOTE: This is not the park for your toddler. There have been perhaps a half dozen injuries over the last 15 years, including a broken leg last year, says the principal of Tuckahoe School next door. But it's one of the more challenging parks for school-aged children, who can use it safely with adequate supervision. Park also includes picnic tables and grills, but no shelter or bathroom facilities. To get there, take I-66 West to Sycamore Street; go right on Sycamore towards Arlington, past two lights. Park is on your left between Lee Highway and 26th Street.*

Maryland

• *Cabin John Regional Park, Tuckerman Lane, Bethesda, 299-4555. This gets our vote as the best playground in the area—five acres of equipment ranging from a fort, Cinderella's carriage, a huge wooden climbing structure, swings, a castle, slides, Indian teepees, and picnic tables. New bathrooms include changing tables, and parents who like to play tennis will appreciate the small tot playground near the courts. Cabin John also has "Noah's Ark" (chickens, cows, etc. to see but not touch) and a tiny train that runs on weekends in April and through the week after Memorial Day to Labor day for a small fee (group rate available). Park open 10 a.m. to sunset; best for children to age 12. To get there, take the Beltway to I-270, take I-270 to the West Democracy Boulevard exit. Go to the first gas station and make a right onto Westlake Drive. Westlake deadends into Tuckerman Lane; take a left, and go to the park entrance.*

• Glen Echo Park, MacArthur Boulevard, Glen Echo, 492-6282. A small park whose wooden climbing structure includes a slide, swings, and a tire swing. The big feature here is a giant teeter-totter that can accommodate several children at once (we counted five at one time), plus a park chock-full of potential stages. The day we were there, we saw impromptu dancing, singing, and puppet shows by child visitors. Glen Echo is home to Adventure Theatre; the playground makes a nice pre- and post-performance way to use extra energy. To get there, take the Beltway to the Carderock/Glen Echo exit, first exit on the Maryland side of the Cabin John Bridge. Follow the signs to Glen Echo; park will be on your left, sharing its parking lot with the Clara Barton House.

• Wheaton Regional Park, Shorefield Drive, Wheaton, 946-7033. Part of a huge complex that includes Brookside Gardens, a nature center, an athletic area with courts for tennis, basketball, handball, baseball and softball, an ice rink, primitive campgrounds and a horseback riding stable, Wheaton has an oldie but goodie playground. It includes one huge, metal climbing and sliding structure for older children, a number

of swings and slides, a good sandbox, and many items that tots find challenging but not scary. It also has Old McDonald's Farm, where you can see (but not pet) chickens, turkeys, ducks, donkeys and goats, and a carousel and train ride, open on weekends in April and daily after Memorial Day until Labor Day. Park open 10 a.m. to sunset; best for children to age 14. To get there, take the Beltway to Georgia Avenue North; go on Georgia to Shorefield Road, turn right and go straight into the park entrance.

Washington
• *Kenilworth Parkside Recreation Center, 4300 Anacostia Drive, N.E., 727-5440. A large, open park including a swimming pool, baseball diamond, amphitheater, and tennis courts, Kenilworth has two playgrounds with things like ripple slides, merry-go-rounds, swings, metal and wooden climbing structures, something that looks like a Swiss cheese for climbing, four concrete dolphins for riding, a circular slide, and some wooden tot swings. To get there, take I-295 North to the Minnesota Avenue/Burroughs exit. Take exit to light, turn left and go back under 295. Go to a four-way stop sign and bear right on Lee Street, past Eastland Gardens. Lee Street will become 40th Street. Turn left into Anacostia Avenue. The park is on Anacostia, to your left.*
• *Chevy Chase Playground, 41st and Livingston Streets, N.W. This is a perfect place to take your toddler and her older sibling. It's fenced off from*

the baseball, basketball, and tennis courts, has a great big sandbox and some nice tot swings, but includes a fantastic roller slide, a tunnel slide, and a "tumble gym" that tips from side to side as you walk up and down it, along with an imaginative metal "car" for driving or climbing. To get there, take Connecticut Avenue north almost to the District line; make a left onto Livingston, and go a few blocks to 41st.

HIKING WITH HALF-PINTS

Ah, a walk through the autumn woods. The cool, crisp air smelling of fall leaves. The multi-colored hue of the forest roof. The sound of woodsy animals scampering around you.

The 35-pound child whining at your foot, begging to be carried.

The expression "take a hike," takes on ominous overtones when you include a tot. Any path that's too long (and for some children we know and are personally related to, this can mean the jog from the car to the house) becomes an exercise in weight-lifting. The term "dawdling" takes on glacial implications. Pockets become receptacles for countless biodegradeable objects, many of which are already biodegrading.

And yet on a pretty fall day, there's really nothing nicer that a walk with your child, is there? The world looks fresh through his eyes, the colors of leaves and the action of fungi are suddenly magical, and stomping on the forest floor to hear the crackles seems like the highest sort of fun.

The key is to keep it short and hook him with something special you're likely to see, anything from five different colors of leaves to a river or a chipmunk. We asked park rangers and recreation people for places like this, each with that extra something—a pond, a farm, a river, a canal. Where possible, we've tried to find parks with something else to fall back on if the walk proves unpopular, like a playground or a nature center.

Along the way, we took counsel from Fairfax Park Authority spokesman Elaine Lussier, who recommended sturdy shoes (well-tied sneakers, for instance) and extra caution around water. She also suggests you take advantage of the kid's tendency to dawdle, stopping often to "look and see and smell and touch and listen," but not collect. Everything in these parks belongs to the park authorities and must stay put.

If you want this to be more of an educational experience but need a little educating yourself first, try the hikes at Rock Creek Park in D.C. or, in Virginia, Riverbend Nature Center in Great Falls and the National Wildlife Federation Center in Vienna. They all have self-guided tours for young children, with interpretive brochures to help you discuss what you're experiencing.

Trying out these parks ourselves, we discovered another great truth: if the day is even dimly warm, bring a picnic. Just a sandwich will do. Everywhere we went had tables or a bench with a lovely view, and we were so smitten with the beauty and peace of the places that it was hard to leave at lunchtime.

You probably already have your own list of favorite walks. Here's ours.

Washington
• *Glover Archbold Trail runs perhaps two miles, all downhill, starting behind the Roy Rogers at*

Van Ness and Wisconsin Avenue. It winds south and southwest toward Foxhall and Reservoir Roads, west of Georgetown University, and is considered "one of the prettiest trails in D.C." by Recreation Department spokesman Earl Elliott. This is for your older tot or school-aged child; beware the climb back up.

* *Kenilworth Aquatic Gardens, Anacostia Avenue and Douglas Street, N.E., 426-6905. This is a park built on the Anacostia marsh, including a half-mile loop trail around 40 ponds filled with plants, turtles, and frogs. A neat trip. Open daily from 7 a.m. to sundown.*

* *Rock Creek Park Nature Center, 5200 Glover Road, N.W., 426-6829. The park contains 24 miles of trails; two short ones near the nature center have interpretive booklets. These, says the naturalist, take 10 to 15 minutes to walk along a wood chip path and point out the forest producers (like trees and shrubs), consumers (turtles and squirrels), and decomposers (fungi and insects), and how they interrelate. You can also catch the Nature Center with its hands-on exhibits and Planetarium show (the one at 1 p.m. is for children age 4 and older). The Nature Center is open Tuesday through Sunday from 9 to 5.*

Maryland

* *Allen's Pond, Route 197 and Northview Drive, Bowie. There's a long (roughly 2½ miles) walk around the pond, which is filled with ducks (bring your own bread crumbs). To get there, go south on*

Route 50 (John Hanson Highway), take the exit to Route 197 South, then turn right onto Northview Drive.

- *Billy Goat Trail, Great Falls, 299-3614. The 1½ mile loop of rocks and cliffs is NOT for your tot. It's designed primarily for billy goats and 10-year-olds, whichever you're herding, but a sturdy 5-year-old may be able to do much of it with your help on a dry day. There are two approaches: one about 25 yards along the canal towpath north of Old Angler's Inn, the other closer to the Visitors Center at Great Falls Park. The Visitors Center (open 9 to 5) has a map for $1, which is worth buying—we've gotten lost on the trail more times than we're willing to admit publicly. And if it looks too daunting, you can always fall back to the towpath for an easy jaunt.*

- *Greenbelt Park, Route 193, Greenbelt, 344-3948. A haven of peace beside the Baltimore-Washington Parkway, Greenbelt has two easy hikes. The half-mile loop called the Azalea Trail, which leads down to a muddy stream bed, is best for your 2- or 3-year-old, but the ¾-mile Dogwood Trail is prettiest in the fall. Stop at the park headquarters for a map. Park open dawn to dusk; headquarters open Monday through Friday from 7 to 4.*

- *Watkins Nature Center, 301 Watkins Park Road, Upper Marlboro, 249-6202. There's a sort-of-a-hike here that runs roughly an eighth of a mile between the Nature Center and the Farm (check the goats, chickens, ducks, sheep, owls, rabbits, geese, and cats), plus a popular playground. A little something* *for every taste. Nature Center open 9 to 4 Monday through Saturday, 11 to 4 Sunday. $5 per car entrance fee for non-Prince George's/Montgomery County residents on weekends in summer.*

Virginia
• *Duff 'N Stuff Trail, Riverbend Nature Center, 8814 Jeffery Road, Great Falls, 759-3211. This is a ¼ mile paved loop designed especially for preschoolers, with eight different stops to look for leaves, rotting logs, shrubs, and fungi. Call ahead and reserve a Discovery Bag, which includes a guidebook, a squirrel puppet, sniff boxes and pictures keyed to posted stations along the trail. The path will take strollers easily. If you bring a picnic, you might want to take it to the Visitors Center down the road, which looks out to the Potomac. Note: the Nature Center has its own entrance, and there is no charge there; but there is a charge at the Visitors Center entrance for non-county residents. Closed Tuesdays; open daily 9 to 5, weekends 12 to 5; closed weekdays January to March.*

• *Paw Paw Passage Trail, 1¼-mile trail for kindergarten children and older located at Riverbend Nature Center, where you can pick up a trail guide. See above for hours and location.*

• *Lake Accotink, 5660 Heming Avenue, Springfield, 569-3464. This is for your older tot—there's a 1½-mile trail at the north end of the lake including an 18-station park course for exercise freaks. The park also has a great playground.*

Hours are dawn to dusk.
* *National Wildlife Federation—Laurel Ridge Conservation/Education Center, 8925 Leesburg Pike, Vienna, 790-4439. A new half-mile paved trail with interpretive signs and bird houses gives tots an idea of what they're looking at and grownups ideas on how to attract wildlife to their own yards. The Education Center's open 8 to 4:30 weekdays; the trail is always open.*
* *Windy Run Park, Kenmore Street, Arlington, no phone. This is a trail of perhaps a mile reaching down through the woods along a stream and ending in a wonderful waterfall where Windy Run spills into the Potomac. There are steps beside the waterfall, but you will probably have to do some toting of tots over the stream here and there. To get there, take the George Washington Parkway to Spout Run Parkway; turn off onto Lorcum Lane, go past the light and halfway down the hill turn right onto Kenmore Street, drive to the end; park in the cul-de-sac.*

TOURING WITH TOTS: A POTPOURRI OF PLACES

So you've just been made Campfire Girls leader/Cub Scout den parent/church youth group organizer/playgroup coordinator. Or, between your children and their friends, you find yourself knee-deep in kids, wondering where to take them.

You'd like to help the impressionable young things take advantage of the many culturally and educationally enriching experiences in this area. You'd also like to get them out of your house. Now what?

There are probably a hundred tours for children's

groups in this area, if you include all the business and store owners willing to troop people behind their scenes. If there's a store—or a firehouse or post office—nearby, you may be able to set something up with just a phone call.

Other places to tour aren't always so obvious, and the best ones tend to be quietly guarded secrets of schoolteachers and Scout leaders. We've dug out a handful of these for you, ranging from a look at robots who sort the mail to a hands-on tour of Jewish history.

One of the very best—a surefire hit complete with dogs, horses, policemen and circus tricks—is given by the U.S. Park Police's Special Forces Branch twice each month in May, June, September, and October. Teachers sign up as much as a year in advance.

Our small contingent got in during early September. Under hundred-foot trees in Rock Creek Park, we watched as a huge, dark German shepherd climbed a ladder, paw over paw, toward a ring of fire waiting for him at the top. He stared, sniffed, and turned around on the narrow walkway to face his master, Officer Gregory Nester of the Park Police's Canine Unit.

At first, it seems the animal can't do it, or at least he won't do it. He looks at his master, turns back to the hoop, turns back to his master, and with a doggy sigh, turns and jumps through the hoop.

Jumping through the fire ring is the ultimate trick from a bagful that includes such stunts as jumping six-foot walls and crawling through 20-foot tunnels. Teaching the dogs to do battle with walls and fire hoops gives them "confidence," Nester says, and shows the dogs that "we won't ask them to do anything they can't do."

Following this latest feat, the crowd goes wild. Thirty or 40 kindergarteners who've signed up for this demonstration from nearby schools shout out "Yay, Doggie!" and beg to pet him.

Petting comes last, after the children meet all the dogs, including Black Bart, a Labrador retriever who's addicted to playing fetch with orange balls. The other thing Bart's crazy about is explosives. Bart spends his days sniffing around the White House grounds, hotel ballrooms, parade routes, and other VIP hangouts, seeking the aromatic whiff of a bomb.

The kindergarten kids have a chance to check Bart's prowess. "I've hidden a bomb on one of these vehicles," says Officer James Bartlett, pointing to the lot where we've all parked, "and Bart's going to help us find it." Nervous titters all around. "It's not a real bomb," he hastens to add, "but it smells like a bomb."

"Will it be on your teacher's car?" one mother asks her group. More nervous titters, as Bart puts nose to bumper, tail wagging. The bomb turns up on one of the park police vehicles, to the children's immense disappointment, and Black Bart sits attentively, waiting for his orange ball reward.

Being an explosives dog is the ultimate in status for the Canine Unit, it seems. All these police dogs, who go home with their officers at night ("I see more of her than I do of my wife," says Nester), go through a 14-week training program to learn the patrol techniques, which include everything from learning to sit at a hand signal to overcoming a fear of the darkness blackening a tunnel that must be traveled.

They get a break for a couple of months because, says Officer James Lynn, some dogs get tired of training. Then follows another six to eight weeks of explosives training. "That way, if it doesn't work out with the explosives, we can always fall back on the patrol training," he explains.

Also on hand for the demonstration are Officer Leon Gray and his horse Frosty, a team that patrols Georgetown's streets six hours a day. Frosty, who "can outrun anything up to a Volkswagen," says Gray, also knows a few fancy steps for the parade grounds. He shows us his finest sidesteps and reverse walking—"something you can't do on a motorcycle," Gray says pointedly.

The animals are definitely the stars of this show; visitors take full advantage of the opportunity to pet them and ask the police questions at the end. For the kids, it's a very different kind of dog-and-pony show.

Here are the details for signing up for the police dog demonstration and a few other tours geared to youngsters. They are free unless otherwise noted.

Washington
• *Special Forces Animal Demonstrations, U.S. Park Police, Rock Creek Park, N.W., 433-1027.*

Demonstrations are given the first and third Thursdays of May, June, September, and October for groups of 10 or more. Phone one to two weeks in advance.

- *U.S. Botanic Gardens, Maryland Avenue and First Street, S.W., 225-8333. With two weeks of advance warning, you can arrange for an hour tour of the garden's tropical and subtropical plants, including the two to three hundred orchids in flower each day, and a room tourists have dubbed "the jungle." There is no lower limit on the number in a group (for school-age kids and older), but very small groups are advised to take the self-guided tour. Tours are Monday through Friday.*
- *B'nai B'rith Klutznick Museum, 1640 Rhode Island Avenue, N.W., 857-6600. A tour of this museum, whose permanent collection shows the life and religious cycle of Jews, includes a hands-on section where children handle a Menorah, Seder plates, spice boxes, and a copy of the Torah. The staff likes two weeks or more advance warning for groups of ten or more from kindergarten age on up. Docents will visit the groups in advance, if asked, to prepare them for the trip. The tours, held every day except Saturday are free, but there's a suggested 50 cent per person donation.*
- *National Gallery of Art, Constitution Avenue and 4th Street, N.W., 842-6249. Volunteer docents can take preschoolers and older children on tours of the collection, offering everything from the Italian Renaissance to the Christmas Story, with special tours for high school classes in math,*

science, history, and literature. One program for fifth-graders includes a 40-minute workshop on technique. Call two weeks in advance for reservations. Tours generally run Monday through Friday, but there are occasional weekend offerings. Preferred group size is 15 to 30.
* *Union Station, 50 Massachusetts Avenue, N.E., 289-2384. Amtrak Police Officer Art Lawson, alias Officer Choo-Choo, takes groups of children from preschool through sixth grade for a puppet show on safety. Participants receive various goodies ranging from coloring books to paper hats. Tours are conducted weekdays for 20 to 30 at a time. Give Lawson at least two weeks' notice.*

Maryland
* *Agricultural Tour, Beltsville Agricultural Research Center, 344-2403. Aimed at the older child (school age and up) and adults, the tour highlights research on plants, sheep, dairy and beef cattle, poultry, swine, nutrition. Most of the tour is conducted aboard a bus but, weather permitting, participants may go into the fields and orchards where things like disease-resistant fruit skins are tested. Groups, which the center defines as "one or more," need to sign up one to three weeks in advance. Tours run Monday through Friday.*
* *Dale Music Company, 8240 Georgia Avenue, Silver Spring, 589-1459. This store holds a unique collection of antique musical instruments—early Mozart bassoons and*

clarinets, all kinds of fiddles and cellos, instruments from Africa and the Middle East. Call Mrs. Warden or Mrs. Burchuk two weeks in advance to set up a tour. They prefer smaller groups.

Virginia
• *Dulles Airport, Chantilly, 471-7838. The airport gives tours Monday through Friday between 10 and noon to kindergarteners and older. The tour includes a short film, a walk through the terminals, and (a great favorite) a ride on the mobile lounge. The staff prefers groups of 10 or more, maximum of 50.*
• *U.S. Postal Service, 8409 Lee Highway, Merrifield, 698-6600. Automatic mail sorters, robotic mail movers and behind-the-scenes mail people are featured in this tour of the 5½-acre facility. Tours for children eight and older are given Monday through Friday, for about an hour; evenings are best. Minimum number: five. Reserve at least two weeks in advance.*
• *Woodlawn Plantation, U.S. Route 1, Mount Vernon, 557-7880. This post-Revolutionary home owned by Nelly Custis Lewis, George Washington's adopted granddaughter, offers tours for everyone from preschoolers to senior citizens. The preschoolers receive a "basket tour," in which a large basket filled with wigs, candles, flax, and other items in daily use during Lewis' time are explained and passed around. At least one week's notice is required. Tour held daily; admission.*

ABOARD THE USS BARRY

"**Y**ou mean we can really come in here?" asks a pre-teen, poking her head into the pilot house of the USS Barry, a decommissioned destroyer now on permanent "visit duty" at the Washington Navy Yard.

The answer is that not only can you come into the pilot house (also known as the bridge), but you can sit in the revolving captain's chair and steer the ship or pull the handle that tells the boys in the engine room to go full speed ahead.

But, as a young sailor on bridge duty explains, "full" is not the fastest speed on the engine-order telegraph. If the lee helmsman pulls the indicator to "full," the throttleman in the engine room steams up to the fastest safe speed. But if the order is "flank," it's damn the torpedoes, the enemy's on our tail, or let's throw caution to the winds and see how fast this tub can really go.

The 424-foot Barry, commissioned in 1956, has a top speed of 33 knots and can carry 22 officers and 315 enlisted men. Although the Barry never had to run for its life from an enemy attack, she has seen action. During the Cuban missile crisis, the ship joined the quarantine force, and during the Vietnam war she served two combat tours and earned two battle stars, performing shore bombardment missions in the Mekong Delta and participating in an amphibious landing near Quang Ngai.

Now, the view from the bridge of the Barry is of the commuter traffic crossing the 11th Street bridge, and the unidentified floating objects in the muddy waters of the Anacostia River are not submarines but flotsam and jetsam. The people shouting "now hear this" through the bull horn and looking into the radar scope are just kids. And though most of them don't know much about naval warfare, they seem to enjoy just being aboard a real ship. The tour is self-guided, so you don't have to delve too deeply into the more arcane aspects of naval technology or decode all the alphabet soup.

And there's lots to decode. There is, for instance, the After Replenishment Station, site of UNREP (underway replenishment) operations—in other words, where the supply helicopters land. Then there's the ASROC (antisubmarine rocket) launcher, which launches RTTs (rocket-thrown torpedoes).

Most kids prefer to skip the official explanations and figure out how the hardware works on their own.

"In the middle of this circle is where they put the rockets and they come out right there," surmises one little girl.

"But then they'd be shooting their own ship," protests another child.

The sailor on deck duty points out that the ASROC launcher, which looks sort of like a tank, can swivel around, crouch or stretch in any direction to get its rockets on target.

In mid-explanation, however, the audience takes off, down a steep, ladder-like stairway to a deck with an enormous gun battery, a station for launching variable-depth sonar devices that bounce sounds back to the destroyer and help it locate submarines, and a launching station for decoy devices that could lure homing torpedoes away from the Barry.

"What if all these torpedoes started flaming up at once?" imagines a child, with undisguised glee.

Well, then, of course, we could take to the boats. In addition to life boats, the Barry, a ship, carries two ship's boats—a motor whaleboat and a captain's gig. Both are used for rescuing downed aviators and persons swept overboard and for taking sailors to shore for liberty when the ship anchors.

After a tour of the Barry, you'd think a kid might remember never to call a ship a boat, since ships carry boats but not vice versa. But other things made a bigger impression.

"Wasn't it neat the way they had windshield wipers in the room where we steered the boat?" asked one child descending the gangplank at tour's end.

Boarding the Barry
• *The USS Barry is open for self-guided tours every day from 10 to 5. It's docked at the Navy Yard, 9th and M Streets, S.E., Washington. Admission is free, but you may be asked to show some identification at the gate. For more informa-*

tion, call 433-3377.

• *You may want to combine a tour of the Barry with a visit to the Navy Memorial Museum, a stone's throw from the gangplank. It has lots of historical items to interest adults, but children love to climb on the anti-aircraft guns and look through the periscope in the simulated submarine. It's open weekends and holidays 10 to 5, weekdays 9 to 5. Call 433-2651.*

DIGGING UP THE PAST

How do you teach archaeology to 10-year-olds? Do you haul them to a museum and trot them through halls filled with chipped pots while you lecture? Do you scrounge through the woods for arrowheads and talk about buffaloes?

While both techniques may work, Steve Shephard, assistant director of a city-funded archaeological research center in Alexandria, Virginia, has a better idea.

Shephard is leery of programs directed at children that involve actual digging at a site: "You can mess up precious archaeological messages from the material's environment if you don't know what you're doing." He prefers, instead, to teach an archaeological approach to culture, encouraging children (and adults) to pick over their living room's "artifacts" and read archaeological messages from their trash piles.

By asking questions about the items found in a present-day home, children learn what kinds of questions archaeologists ask and why. By going through a trash pile, children can figure out what sort of food the occupants consumed. They might find evidence of "tools" for everyday living.

Looking around a home, the cultural explorers can learn about a family's possessions, and what the standard of living might have been. These are the questions archaeologists ask as they uncover ancient sites.

A group of children from our neighborhood recently focused their archaeological eyes on two cultures, our own and one from the past. We drove to the Claude Moore Colonial Farm at Turkey Run, which demonstrates a poor, backwater operation of the late eighteenth century mode of life in McLean, Virginia.

Here the children peered into the potato cellar, scurried after unfenced chickens, and listed garden vegetables as barefoot, grubby rangers patiently answered their many questions.

After noting some obvious differences between our material cultures—acres of farm vs. quarter-acre lots, a tobacco-drying barn vs. a garage, edible animals vs. pets—the children answered a question that graphically demonstrated the gap between these lifestyles.

We went to count the farm children's possessions and found only three. The one-room log cabin holds a blanket, a pair of shoes, and an extra shirt for each inhabitant. This contrasts strongly with our own He-man, blue jeans and book-strewn bedrooms, where literally hundreds of items serve no survival role.

Another major disparity emerged when our 10-year-old spokesman, Sherry, started looking for the trash. "We don't have any," a wood-chopping ranger informed us. "If it's edible, we feed it to the hogs; if it's not, we burn it; if it breaks, we fix it; if it tears, we mend it."

"Gee, we're really wasteful," Sherry commented.

A question that puzzled the children at home, how to date the site, became even more mind-boggling at Turkey Run. Shephard had given us a hint: look in fencepost holes and date whatever dropped into them when the fence was built.

Lori, 13, wryly observed that our non-biodegradable plastic toys and fast-food hamburger containers will outlive us. She thinks future archaeologists will date us as part of the "plastic people."

But how do you date an eighteenth century site operating in the twentieth century? Eight-year-old Wendy, an even-keeled, straightforward towhead, thinks that "this will be really confusing to some poor archaeologist, with the log cabin and everybody's candy wrappers in the same place."

Our featherweight archaeologists sidestepped such confusion by using the culture's living examples to answer questions, and soon their lists filled out.

Then, as we piled back into the car, the kids groped toward some complex conclusions. We started with a simple question: What would we be like if we grew up without toys?

"Pretty dull," Wendy retorted.

Our carful concluded that Turkey Run's children had no toys because they had no time to play or go to school; they had to help their parents instead. Ten-year-old Debbie tied this to our wastefulness. "We've thought up all these machines that do our work for us, so we have lots of extra time to do unnecessary stuff," she analyzed. "Like go to school," she teased.

"Those kids went to school in a way," Lori protested. "Their parents taught them to sew, and farm crops, and make stuff."

So when the children grew up, what would they be educated to do?

"Farm," came the chorus.

Is the farm poor, or rich? "Poor," they moaned.

So what would the kids be when they grew up? "Oh," came Debbie's tentative conclusion, "they would be poor."

And what would the children's children be?

"They could go to school and learn something else," insisted Sherry, our resident optimist.

Like the children in our car? "Yeah," came the uncertain replies.

My daughter, then 6, was silent throughout this discussion, but it evidently gave her pause. That night, as we made up round sandwiches for a picnic the next day, we wondered aloud what to do with the unused bread crumbs. Emma suggested that we take them back to Turkey Run, "to feed the poor people." She also thought we might bring some of her 643 unnecessary possessions, so their kids won't grow up poor.

Digging into Virginia's Past
• *Alexandria Archaeology Office, Torpedo Factory Arts Center, 105 North Union Street, Alexandria, 838-4399. Small museum showing local artifacts, open Tuesday through Saturday from 10 to 5. Use*

volunteers age 15 and up in year-round digs.
* *Claude Moore Colonial Farm at Turkey Run, 6310 Old Georgetown Pike, McLean, near the intersection of Route 193 and Route 123, 442-7557. Open Wednesday through Sunday from 10 to 4:30. Admission. A 1771 lower-class, 12-acre farm, where the family prepares and eats a noon-day meal. Special programs on the first Saturday of each month from 1 to 4. (For more on the Colonial Farm, see Living in the Past chapter).*
* *Fairfax Archaeology Office Lab, 2855 Annandale Road, Falls Church, 237-4881. The lab, located in the James Lee School on the 2nd floor, is open Tuesday through Friday from 8 to 4:30, plus occasional evenings. Parents and teenage children welcome to assist the archaeologist each Saturday; meet at the lab at 8 a.m. Office currently working on a variety of ancient Indian sites. They also run a field school in the summer for nine days; sign up through this office.*
* *Summer Enrichment Program in Archaeology, Fairfax County Public Schools, Lacy Instruction Center, 698-7500. This is a one-credit course that takes kids eighth grade and older from around the Washington Metropolitan area on digs. Call around the beginning of May to get on the list.*

CRUISING CLOPPER LAKE

"This is what was here before all the people and the fast food restaurants and the shopping malls got here," says naturalist Pete Schrantz.

We're in the middle of 90-acre Clopper Lake on an electric pontoon boat called the Blue Heron. Schrantz, a Gaithersburg native and part-time ranger at Seneca Creek State Park, is showing us the Gaithersburg that was.

"This is a man-made lake," he explains to the five adults and seven children aboard. "What they did here was similar to what a beaver would do. They dammed up the creek system with a big piece of earth. They rounded it up to stop the water, and the lake has been filling up since 1976."

The boat's electric motor purrs very quietly, but Schrantz sometimes turns it off, the better to see wildlife.

"We have foxes, raccoons, white-tailed deer, possums..."

"Do you have rabbits?" interrupts a little girl.

"Lots," answers the guide. "And groundhogs so big that sometimes kids think they're grizzly bears and come back and tell us that we have bears in the park!"

But on this particular afternoon we see nary a bear, only a fisherman in a folding chair on the bank.

"There are bluegills and bass in the lake," says Schrantz. "You're almost guaranteed to catch a bluegill, even fishing from the dock with a piece of bread for bait. But the adult fishermen are after largemouth bass."

We cruise to a spot where a meadow borders the lake, "a beautiful place for grazing deer and fox dens," according to Schrantz.

As we scan the grass, wood ducks ruffle the meadow and fly up toward the woods.

"Those tiny ducks live in holes in the trees," Schrantz tells us. "But there aren't enough places for them to live, so we supplement the housing supply by putting out wooden nesting boxes for them. They're migratory, but they're not migrating yet. The young have just gotten their wings, and this is a testing period."

Schrantz wants to cruise into a cove where dead black trees are sticking up through the water. The blue heron, the big waterbird that gave its name to our boat, likes to hide here. But so do the bass, and out of consideration for a boat full of fishermen, we retreat.

"There are 150 species of birds in the park. Earlier in the year you couldn't go anywhere without bumping into somebody with binoculars. This is usually a good place to see the great blue heron," he says cutting off the motor.

"How big is it?" asks a child.

"About 3½ feet tall, bigger than you," answers the guide. "It's slate blue and has long, skinny legs."

What we see, however, is the blue heron in miniature: a green heron, with a fish in its mouth, flies just above the water near our boat.

"See him!" cries Schrantz. "He uses his bill like a sword to spear the fish, and he has a little tuft on his head that he raises when he flies."

We pass an old pine plantation, a remnant of the days when part of the park was a farm, and Schrantz points to it approvingly.

"The pines attract a different species of birds, such as woodpeckers. Deer also like a little pine in their diet," he says. "There are watersnakes in the lake, but no water moccasins. And on a hot sunny day, you'd see a lot of turtles lounging on the rocks."

We have almost circumnavigated the lake. Before returning to the boathouse, Schrantz stops for a last look for wildlife.

"Be very quiet and see how many bird songs you hear," he urges.

"You gotta be quiet so the ducks don't get scared," a child whispers to her little sister.

Someone hears a cricket.

"This is a big time as far as insects are concerned," says the guide. "And did you hear that chirpy-chirpy sound? That was a chipmunk."

Suddenly, a high pitched whoop pierces the silence, a cry distinctly human and expressing great joy.

"Someone caught a fish," surmises Schrantz.

Cruises etc. at Seneca Creek State Park
* *To get to the park, take I-270 to the Montgomery Village exit and follow Quince Orchard Road to Clopper Road. Turn right on Clopper Road to the park entrance at 11950. There is an entrance fee. The 60,000-acre park has hiking trails and an orienteering course as well as cruises on the electric boat. Canoes, rowboats, pedalboats, and sailboats are also available for rent. Call 924-2127.*

WAVE POOLS: SURF ON TAP

Do you crave the waves? Want to go with the flow? Ride the tide?

If it's just wave action you're after—if you can skip the salt air, fabulous french fries and ticky tacky wacky boardwalk—there's a way to get it without crawling across the Bay Bridge. Two nearby wave pools (three, if you count the one close to Williamsburg) are perfect for people who like their surf on tap.

At a wave pool the fresh water peaks and crashes in a ten-minute fury of fun, described by one waverider as a "liquid trampoline." Tiny children toddle near the breakers' edge while their older siblings body surf or ride the waves on rafts, and parents bob serenely at the deep end. When the waves stop, the population shifts, young children wade out deeper into now-calm waters, and teens, leaping over the sides, head for the water slides and snack bars nearby.

Developed from German technology, wave pools are a relatively recent American phenomenon. "Europe itself already has over 200 such pools, most of them enclosed," says Don Steele, president of WaveTek, the company supplying most American wave pool technology. "We're really kind of behind the times."

Introduced in 1970 in Alabama, the pools now flow in 60 or 70 locations throughout the U.S.,

Steele says. In some places, such as Wild World in Largo, Maryland, they're the "hark of the park," he says, the chief draw in a place that also includes fast food/fast ride/hard sell ways to spend your money.

In other places, such as Cameron Run Park in Alexandria, the pool is a profit-making enterprise that puts money into park coffers. "This pays for things like nature walks and special programs in other parks," says Paul McCray, manager of the pool park, which is part of the Northern Virginia Regional Park Authority.

Cameron Run, at 17,400 square feet, is small compared with Wild World's 45,000 square feet. That expanse, nearly an acre, makes it one of the world's largest wave pools. But it's still only half

the size of number one, Big Surf, Arizona's 98,000-square-foot wave pool called a Tsunami.

On the other hand, the waves are the same wherever you go. At Cameron Run and Wild World, officials say, the waves shoot up to four feet high ("make that 3½ feet," one lifeguard says), on top of a maximum depth of eight feet.

"People always ask us what makes the waves," says lifeguard Robert Albarado at Wild World. "They think we shake the pool, or the bars at the end wiggle, or something."

Fact is that the waves come from a row of almost idiotically simple machines that line the back of the pool. Sixty-horsepower engines drive huge, black airhoses that shift between blowing out air and sucking it in. These fans—eight at Wild World, four at Cameron Run—alternate their "breathing," and together they create air pockets that push and pull the water into giant waves.

"In some ways, it's like being in the middle of the ocean in rough water," says Albarado. "The waves come really fast and you can't stand up."

On the other hand, says McCray at Cameron Run, "there's no undertow, and we do turn the waves off every ten minutes," something you don't find at too many oceans.

But is it safe? "Our safety record is excellent compared to ordinary swimming pools," says Steele. There have been three wave-pool drownings reported over the last 15 years, including a 9-year-old boy who drowned at Wild World in 1983.

But there are no comparative statistics stacking

the five dozen wave pools against the thousands of below-ground public swimming pools, points out Joyce Coonley of the National Injury Information Clearinghouse. Her records show some two dozen deaths in such pools in 1984, as opposed to zero for wave pools. "They really are two different things entirely," she says. "Wave pools are classified as amusement rides."

Managers at the wave pools point with pride to the extraordinary lengths to which they go to ensure public safety. For instance, the guards, who must meet more rigorous standards than for most pools, all know cardiopulmonary resuscitation. McCray describes the lifeguarding as "very intense, the equivalent of ocean guarding."

But even with that, Jean'yves Ghazi, head of Wild World's lifeguarding section, thinks "public education... needs to be improved. People are not educated about this kind of water, and don't realize that water makes them tired."

He, and others, offer the following advice for those visiting a wave pool:

Never leave small children or nonswimmers unguarded. "We'll have parents dropping off their little ones at the pool and then going to take rides," says Wild World spokesman Amy Ryan, with horror. "You just can't leave them safely."

Weak or inexperienced swimmers should stay behind the four-foot depth mark, shown clearly on the bottom or side of the pool. "Anything beyond four feet is really dangerous water for most children," McCray says, "because if a wave knocks them down, they can't stand up."

Take frequent breaks. Most wave pools enforce a 10- to 15-minute break every hour, in which, Ghazi advises, you should "stay out of the water and the sun. The combination of sun and water really depletes your energy."

Drink plenty of liquids. "Swimming is dehydrating," Ghazi advises—something that's also true of sunbathing.

Be wary of rafts. "They can give you a false sense of confidence," McCray says, "and make you feel safe beyond your depth." Rafts are only for experienced swimmers, wave pool managers agree.

Put life vests on young children. These are available free of charge at Wild World, but not at Cameron Run. "It's the same as rafts," McCray says. "A life vest can give you a false sense of confidence." Children of the age or experience to need a life vest should be securely guarded by a parent, he says.

Where the Wave Pools Are

• *Cameron Run Regional Park, 4001 Eisenhower Avenue, Alexandria, 960-0767. Park includes 17,400-square-foot wave pool, three waterslides, and a baby pool. Open every day from 10 to 8. Admission varies with age and time. Season passes and volume discounts available. Take Capital Beltway to the Telegraph Road Exit, follow the brown signs to the park.*
• *Water Country, P.O. Box 3088, Williamsburg, (804) 229-9300. Park includes a 24,000-square-foot*

wave pool, six waterslides, two inner-tube rides (one slow, one fast), two activities pools (one for young children), and a diving show. Admission varies, children under 4 free. Take I-95 to Richmond, take I-64 to Williamsburg, get off at Exit 57B. Go ¼ mile north, park is on right.

* *Wild World, 13710 Central Avenue, Largo, 249-1500. Park includes Wild Wave, a 45,000-square-foot wave pool, seven water slides, and a large, shallow pool with activities for young children. Admission varies with age and time, also entitles you to the park's other rides, shows, games, and children's park. Take the Capital Beltway to Exit 15A and stay on Route 214 to the park.*

FEEDING THE DUCKS

For younger kids, a Saturday spent feeding the ducks can be as entertaining as a Saturday watching Donald Duck cartoons. It makes a pleasantly nostalgic outing for parents, too, and it's low budget. All you need is some hard bread or soft crackers and a few hungry ducks.

The District, oddly enough, has the most country-like, ecologically sound ducks, but if they're hungry enough they'll eat your bread anyway.

The pond at the National Arboretum, a 400-acre tract at Bladensburg Road and New York Avenue,

N.E., provides an idyllic pastoral setting for feeding the mixed flock of ducks and geese. But better not cast your bread upon the waters until the waterfowl are right there; the pond also contains some voracious fish who may snap up the goodies first.

When you run out of duck food, there's a miniature Greek temple beside the pond that kids love to play house in. Picnicking is not allowed except in a designated picnic ground, but no one will object if the kids munch on the stuff that was meant for the ducks.

Another good place to feed the ducks in town is Constitution Gardens, which hosts migrating ducks attracted by the natural plantings around the pond. National Park Service officials don't really encourage supplementing the waterfowl diet with processed food, but the ducks probably won't mind a bit.

Ducks, herons, egrets, and other waterfowl also flock to the Roaches Run Waterfowl Sanctuary, located right beside the southbound lane of the George Washington Parkway just north of National Airport.

Between the din of the highway and the roar of the planes, neither you nor the ducks will be able to hear the kids' cries of "quack, quack."

The sanctuary sprawls over a large area, and there is a lot of tall marsh grass for the waterfowl to retreat into. While I threw some bread into the water and waited for the ducks to get the message, my 4-year-old and her friend had fun gathering feathers from the ground. When some ducks appeared, a middle-aged couple, probably serious waterfowl watchers, put out bird seed for them. I felt definitely outclassed as we emptied our polka-dotted bag of stale Wonder Bread. Naturalists recommend bird seed rather than bread for ducks. Bird seed costs more than leftovers, but it would provide a golden opportunity for the standard nutrition lecture.

In Fairfax County, both Burke Lake (non-resident entrance fee) and Lake Accotink have ducks in residence. A smaller, lesser known but lovely duck pond is located in E.C. Lawrence Park in Centerville (take I-66 to Sully Road, Route 28; take the first right turn into Walney Road and follow it to the park). The ducks here greeted us enthusiastically, quacking in anticipation before we even got out of the parking lot.

We also got a warm reception from the ducks at Louise F. Cosca Regional Park in Clinton. (From the Beltway, take Branch Avenue, Route 5, to Old Branch Avenue, which becomes Brandywine Road. Follow Brandywine Road to Thrift Road and turn right to the park entrance. Follow signs to the parking lot for picnic area A).

Between the parking lot and the 15-acre lake where the ducks hang out lies a wooded play area with such irresistible attractions as metal Indian teepees and forts. When the kids have exhausted all possibilities, lead them toward the lake. There's a resident flock of mallards, muscovies, domestic whites, and many odd ducks that illustrate the wonders of cross breeding, which can provide a lead-in for a discussion of genetics if you really feel up to it.

EXPLORING AN ESTUARY

We are meandering around a meander in quiet Muddy Creek, where the only sounds are the ripple off our canoe paddles in the water, the flute-like call of the marsh wren, and the voice of our guide, ecologist Dennis Whigham.

"That's the narrow-leaf cattail, the only kind that can stand salt water," he says. "Cattails turn brown in late August, but the dead shoots are essential to get oxygen down to the roots. If the muskrats chew off the shoots, the plant won't grow. There's a small moth that comes into the flowering heads of the cattails. It eats the seeds and spins a web that keeps the whole mass together."

What happens in an estuary, a place where fresh water meets salt water, is one of the things scientists study at the Smithsonian Environmental Research Center, a 2,600-acre preserve in Edgewater, Maryland. They give the public a peek at the wonderful world of wetlands in two-hour canoe expeditions and on guided walks, both of which are available free by pre-arrangement.

"Now we'll start working our way down the gradient," says Whigham, leading our convoy of 13 life-vest-clad people in six canoes downstream, toward the place where Muddy Creek meets the Rhode River, an arm of the Chesapeake Bay. The cattails are bending in the breeze, and some cattail shoots are floating in the water, a sure sign that there are muskrats around. The creek hosts an active muskrat lodge (which looks like a pile of brush), and river otters live in holes dug out of the creek banks.

The scientists, too, have built structures in the estuary—not homes, but a device that measures the flow of water, and a fish weir, a V-shaped trap that temporarily detains the fish swimming either upstream or downstream.

"We can document the movement of the fish," explains Whigham. "They come into the creek to breed, and the young fish stay to feed. Marshes are incredibly important as places where fish raise their young, find shelter from predators, and get nutrition."

Silverside minnows and pumpkinseed sunfish live in the creek full time. White perch come to spawn, and blue crabs come to molt. Smithsonian scientists attach ultrasound devices to some of the crabs to track their movements. Another device registers every time a crab chews, recording exactly how many bites it takes the crab to devour a clam.

Below the fish weir, the creek that began as a freshwater stream with the forest at the bank gives way to salt marshes and tidal flats, and here the canoes turn back. The return trip is upstream, but tide and wind are in our favor.

"Quite often we see kingfishers and, once in a while, a bald eagle," says Whigham. "And there's a tree swallow; you can see a flash of white belly. We have a pair of red tails (hawks) that breed here and a lot of marsh wrens. They cut off cattail shoots to weave nests, and they usually build four or five fake nests, too, to keep predators away from the real nest."

Later, back on dry—or mostly dry—land, we see the estuary from a terrestrial point of view with ecologist Jim Lynch on a 1½-mile journey down the Discovery Trail. The trail leads through several environments, from forest to marsh.

We start at what Lynch calls an old field, a pasture abandoned about 40 years ago. By rights, the area should have been reforested by now, but reforestation has been thwarted by vines.

"When we think of competition, we think of animals and birds, but plants fight it out for food and water, too," says Lynch, pointing out honeysuckle, wild grape, Virginia creeper, and the thick, hairy vines of poison ivy.

In another place on the trail, the forest has begun the process of succession—regenerating in what was originally forest, but has been cleared for farming. The first trees to succeed are pioneering trees, such as tulip poplar and black cherry, trees that grow fast and need a lot of light. Further on, the forest canopy grows thicker, allowing only dappled light to fall on the trail. This, says Lynch, is a mature forest, where hardwoods such as oak and hickory have replaced the pioneering trees, which can't get enough light.

From the dark, cool forest, we emerge into blinding sunlight and follow a raised boardwalk across Hog Island Marsh.

"The greenbriar here is a favorite browse for deer," says Lynch. "You can see the woody plants being replaced by grasses. The last trees to go are the willow oaks. In colonial times, salt marsh hay was used for fodder. It's a big, floating mat of vegetation, like a big peat bog. You can see trails made by the muskrats through the marsh."

The trail also takes us past evidence of human incursions into the environment. There is a computerized field weather station, for example, which charts temperature, humidity, wind speed, sunlight, and other variables. There are boxes left by the scientists to collect leaves. There is also evidence of less scientific human activity.

"They're such tempting targets," laments Lynch, as we gather around a thick beech tree carved with every combination of letters in the alphabet. "I've never seen a beech tree not covered with initials."

Outdoor Adventures with the Smithsonian
- *The Smithsonian Environmental Research Center offers canoe trips seven days a week, spring through fall. No canoeing experience is necessary, but paddlers must be 12 years or over. Children between 8 and 12 may be canoe passengers.*
- *Guided Discovery Trail walks are available seven days a week, year round. Children should be 10 or older. Reservations are necessary for both activities. For reservations, information, and directions, call (301) 798-4424.*

A SWAMP WITH KNEES

The small group is experiencing Battle Creek Cypress Swamp at its swampiest. Spring rain is plopping into limpid pools, marring the mirror image of the bald cypress trees that merge into a cathedral ceiling 150 feet overhead. Sneakers squeak on the wet boardwalk that naturalist Dwight Williams built through the swamp, which is owned by the Nature Conservancy. Battle Creek, the small stream that feeds the swamp, gurgles with rainpower. And the cypress "knees," cinnamon-colored roots that rise four feet out of the water, are shiny-wet.

The rambling roots, or knees, are one of nature's riddles. Scientists once believed they were snorkels that help the trees breathe. Now the prevailing

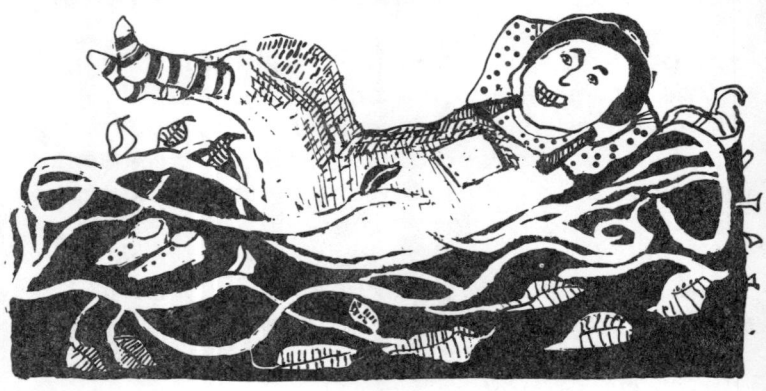

theory is that the knees help stabilize the tree in its boggy foundation. Even the fact that the swamp is where it is—Calvert County, Maryland—is a bit of a mystery. Bald cypress stands are common in the south, but rare this far north, and the site is a national historic landmark.

The bald cypress is the only conifer that sheds its foliage—tiny, lacy leaves and the branchlets that hold them. The canopy of leaves closes over in May, Williams says, but even without it the visitor can spot no birds but only hear the shrill, staccato call of the tufted titmouse.

"Warblers are the main migrants we get here," says Williams, "and there are a lot of woodpeckers. By May, there'll be wildflowers around the trail, especially violets, spring beauties, and bloodroot."

To See the Knees
- *To get to Battle Creek Cypress Swamp Sanctuary, take Maryland Route 4 (Pennsylvania Avenue Extended) through Prince Frederick. Turn right on Route 506, then left on Grays Road to the sanctuary. Adjacent to the sanctuary is a nature center that sponsors nature walks and other activities. For information, call (301) 535-5327.*

TAME WAYS TO THE WILD

On a gorgeous, sunny summer day, a brush-footed butterfly opened her wings, soaked up the solar power she uses to help her fly, and took off across the meadow of Silver Spring's Maydale Nature Center. In hot pursuit ran a crew of tots, preteens, net carriers, and a naturalist holding a bug jar. She never had a chance.

Carrying their captive, the pursuers continued their mission: to seek out and explore new butterflies; to figure out what they were eating (nectar), where they were going (to the flowers), and why they hold their wings in that funny way while parking on a flower (to regulate body temperature). All this and more was uncovered during the hour-long program, one of dozens scheduled for families in nature centers around the city.

Good places to hang out on a slow summer or deadly winter day, nature centers, with their arrowheads, turtles, ponds, marshes, woods, and hiking trails, offer low-key introductions to natural treasures. In addition to the usual looks at bats, bugs, and beavers, area nature centers take visitors on hunts for natural foods, show them how to build bird feeders and make corn husk dolls, and use blindfolds to help them learn about their other senses.

Not all of these programs take place at the

centers themselves. Hidden Pond Nature Center in Springfield, Virginia, for example, takes its shows on the road to Fairfax's Burke Lake Park during the summer. We followed them on a Friday night, and saw a naturalist carrying a beaver pelt. She led us, along with 20 other campers and visitors, in search of a live animal with pelt intact.

"Look, Daddy, the moon is following us," whispered a young tot as we wandered in the dark toward the 218-acre, man-made lake. The night was sweet, the air relatively clear of mosquitoes, and—for those of us used to spending the evening behind double-locked doors—the experience of walking unmolested through a dark wood was a wonder worth repeating.

Although they're naturally nocturnal, the beavers apparently didn't share our enthusiasm for communing; they dived into their dens before we hit shore. "I tell you what, folks," said the naturalist in a somewhat apologetic voice, "if you want to see beaver lodges and a dam, go to Huntley Meadows."

She was right. But beaver dams aren't the only reason to go to this, our family's favorite center. At Huntley Meadows in Hybla Valley, more than a mile of boardwalk roams through a marshland that is alive with swamp roses and beaver and muskrat lodges, and filled with the booming of bullfrogs and more exotic birds than watchers say can be found almost anywhere else around D.C.

"I guess the most exciting bird I've seen is the glossy ibis," says naturalist Randy Legge. "But scarlet tanagers are also common; they're a pretty bird," he says, pointing to a plump red bird with black wings in his birding guide.

We're standing atop a wooden tower that overlooks the beaver dam, where visitors can get an eyeful of the busy life below. Pointing to the beaver lodges (three of them within spitting distance of the tower), Legge says he's often seen ducks and geese resting and even nesting on top. "It's high up for the marsh," he explains, "so they can get a good view, and it's completely safe (for the birds) since beavers are herbivorous."

Not all animals in the park have such vegetarian tastes, of course. "The droppings along the boardwalk are from otters," says Legge. "If you look closely, which most people don't, you can see that they're ground-up crayfish."

"Oh, gross," says Bryce, age 8.

He and a friend had been wading in a pool where the boardwalk sags below water level until "some lady told us there are snakes in there, Mom, and we didn't want to get bitten."

In fact, no poisonous snakes have been found at Huntley Meadows. Other than the mosquitoes and poison ivy that are the hazards of backyards everywhere, nature centers offer one of the tamest approaches going to the wild—a great place to dive in to the out of doors.

Natural Doings
• *Newsletters and flyers listing upcoming activities are available at your local nature center*

and library. Most centers offer weekly programs throughout the summer, monthly throughout the year. Centers in Fairfax and Arlington run nature camps in the summer; call in late spring for sign up.

* *The parks mentioned above are: Hidden Pond Nature Center, 8511 Greeley Boulevard, Springfield, Virginia, 451-9588; Huntley Meadows Park, 3701 Lockheed Boulevard, Hybla Valley, Virginia, 768-2525; and Maydale Nature Center, 1726 Briggs Chaney Road, Silver Spring, Maryland, 384-9447.*

BIRDING FOR BEGINNERS

In the fall woods, between the C & O Canal and the Potomac River, a dozen adults and twice as many kids huddle together, making a sound that sounds like "pish." They've spotted a bird called a flicker in a tree and are trying to "pish" it down.

"Pishing is one of the really fun things you can do," says Rich Bray of the Audubon Naturalist Society, who is introducing a troop of neophytes to birding. What we're doing, he explains, is imitating a bird's distress call. When other birds hear it they think one of their comrades is in trouble, so they come down to where birders can watch and identify them.

Identification is the hard part for neophytes.

"I picked up the field guide and it just opened to the flicker," says a neophyte with beginner's luck. "But how would I have identified it otherwise?"

"You'll develop some discrimination," Bray assures him. I went through the guide and marked some birds I hoped to see. Peterson recommends just leafing through the guide. Pretty soon you'll get a feel for the different families.

To get us used to the guides, naturalist Neal Fitzpatrick has us go through and find a bird that's yellow (Lawrence's warbler or a yellow rail); a bird with really long wings (a heron or plover); and a bird with a yellow eye (a herring gull). We also learn to adjust binoculars by focusing on some stuffed birds the naturalists have brought along. But now we're faced with the real thing: live birds flying past in such rapid succession that before we can identify one, another has grabbed our attention.

"It's brown, sort of, with black wings," 6-year-old Reece describes a bird that's crossing the Potomac to Virginia.

"Twelve o'clock in the big sycamore tree, what is it?" shouts someone else.

"Has it got a speckled breast?" Bray asks a boy who is perched on his father's shoulders.

"What's going across the river now?" asks Fitzpatrick. "See that undulating flight—and it's got white on its back, a perfect field mark. Look under woodpeckers," he adds, giving it away as a common flicker.

By the time the sky clears briefly, we've seen a heron, an osprey, ducks, chickadees, thrushes, and a warbler.

Identifying birds on the wing is a skill acquired and sharpened through observation and practice. One way to acquire this skill, Fitzpatrick suggests, is to set up a backyard bird feeder and get to know the birds that visit. Another way is to use your ears—to get to know birds by their chipping and singing.

"For the next fifty seconds, count the number of bird songs you can hear," says Bray. "I heard about 40 chips from about four different species," he says when time's up. "They called about 40 different times but the calls were what we call chips, not songs like you hear in the spring. What is it they're doing in spring that makes them sing?"

"Courting," offers one child.

"Mating," offers another.

"And having babies," pipes up a third child

Since the kids seem to know all about the sex lives of birds, Fitzpatrick pulls out jars of stuff that show other things about birds, such as pigeon wings and bird skulls.

"Birds have holes in their skulls and in all of their bones," he says as the kids pass the skull around. "This makes birds very light."

"They're probably as light as the floating princess in my book, but she wasn't a bird," comments 5-year-old Kate.

Meanwhile, Margy, 14, has spotted some vultures.

"How are they holding their wings?" asks Bray.

"They're holding them up, they're soaring!" she answers.

"That makes a big difference when you're vulture watching," Bray tells her, "If they're soaring, they're probably turkey vultures."

"Look at the petrol hawk!" shouts Fitzpatrick, and we all dive into our field guides. But in a few seconds the roar in the sky makes us look up and laugh at the joke. An airplane is flying overhead.

If we're consummate amateurs (and who else would fall for a gag like that?) the Audubon Society wants us to see what some experienced birders are doing, and we carpool to the Adventure Bird

Banding Station to meet Margaret Donnald, a volunteer who has banded thousands of birds.

The birds fly into fine, invisible nets and are put into bags to be banded.

"Hey, there are birds in those bags, and in that box," says Reece, and Donnald takes the birds out one by one to show them to us and explain the banding process.

"Hi," she greets a catbird that's already been banded. "He's a young catbird, just born this summer. His eye is a dull grey-brown. When he's an adult, he'll have a deep purple eye."

When she releases the bird, it flies toward us, and everybody ducks.

"Oh, I like that one," says a little girl, but attention is already riveted on the next bird, a Swainson's thrush.

"He's been eating spicebush berries. You can tell by the orange on his stomach," says Donnald, blowing the feathers apart to show the fat underneath. "As soon as the weather is right, he'll take off, so he has to put on some fat."

A tiny black-throated warbler is next, and to determine its age Donnald looks at its skull with a magnifying glass to see if it's ossified. Noting the age and weight, which will eventually be fed to a Department of Interior computer, she uses a pair of small pliers to fasten a numbered band around the bird's leg.

"It doesn't hurt," she assures the kids. "It doesn't even touch the bird."

The next bird to be banded is a myrtle warbler,

and at the end of the process Donnald turns the bird over and puts it on its back in the outstretched hands of 8-year-old Janet. The bird is so calm and the girl's hands so still that it seems as if the warbler will stay forever.

"Maybe he's taking a nap," another kid suggests, and when the bird finally takes off, Janet is the envy of all.

"Feel my hand, mom," she exclaims. "It's still hot!"

Getting to Know Birds
• *For information about Audubon Naturalist Society birding expeditions for families, call 652-5965.*

America grew up as a rural farming community, but chances are your children are growing up now with no personal knowledge of what it means to farm. We can fix that with four living history projects rimming the Beltway, family farms that give you a chore's-eye-view of just what it means to be tied to the land.

Oxon Hill Farm, once the source of food for St. Elizabeth's Hospital, is set up by the National Parks to show farming at the start of the industrial

age. Its aim is to depict the way it was in the late nineteenth and early twentieth centuries, when "horse-drawn machinery was at its peak," says Park Ranger Jim Rosenstock.

That means the wheat thresher, corn sheller, clip saw, and hay baler had to be scrounged from antique auctions and old family farms. "Most places that have been operating for awhile have these things rusting in the fields," Rosenstock says. And the horses they're hooked to, big-footed Belgian draft animals, are as rare as the machines they pull.

It also means that rangers are in costume, and the animals—pigs, goats, cows, chickens, turkeys, ducks, rabbits, sheep, horses, burros, and ponies—and crops are true to the period; you'll find no soy beans and raddichio growing her.

But Rosenstock admits that they take liberties with the historical side, like using modern tractors to pull the hayrides. And "some of the recreational things are not pure history," he says.

Still, the basic idea taught here is as true today as it was historically: that "everybody is dependent on agriculture," says Rosenstock. "It's easy to get away from the concept when we buy everything wrapped in plastic at the grocery store," he thinks.

Then there are more elementary lessons, like animal identification. "We still get kids who point at the horses and say, Big Dog," he says. "Or they watch me milk the cows and can't quite grasp the idea that something from a big, living, moving, breathing animal is the same stuff they get out of the refrigerator every day. They say, 'yuk! I never want to drink milk again.'"

But some are really enthralled by it, he adds, and like to try the milking process themselves.

If your kids are udderly educated already and you're looking for more history, farms in the area offer a nearly consecutive view of the last 300 years. Start with the authentic, pre-Revolutionary, "poor folks" on the Claude Moore Colonial Farm at Turkey Run, near McLean, Virginia.

Here a "family" faces life on 12 acres without irrigation, a demonstration which yielded exactly 16 ears of corn after one summer's drought, they say. On the first Saturday of each month, they have special demonstrations (like fat rendering or candle dipping), and their Harvest Festival comes mid-fall.

Further up the economic scale is National Colonial Farm in Accokeek, across from Mt. Vernon. This is designed as a 1752 tobacco plantation, which means that "it's middle class; not very exciting, but a real contrast to Mt. Vernon," says a spokesman. They run special historical programs, too. In fall of 1986 they held a funeral ("we did weddings two years in a row and were looking for something different"), complete with coffin, lengthy religious ceremony ("it makes the Catholic Mass look like nothing"), burial, huge meal, and the custom of passing out rings and gloves "to pay honor to the deceased."

Oxon Hill Farm is the next chunk in time—1898 to 1914, they say—followed by Frying Pan Farm Park in Fairfax. Here, they show "what a family subsistence farm was like in Fairfax in the 1920s to 1940s," says a spokesman. That means the horses are still doing the pulling, only 15 acres are in crops, and life revolves around the needs of cows and chickens. Frying Pan schedules "chores tours" in advance for groups, if you've got a Scout troop and need something different to do with them.

"We get a lot of people here who came from a farm background, or were raised on a farm as a child and now want to show their children what it was like," says Rosenstock of Oxon Hill Farm. "But really, I think they come for themselves," he says.

"People just want to get away from the craziness of city life, and spend an hour of peacefulness out here," he suspects. At Oxon Hill Farm, you can watch the pre-Thanksgiving turkeys ruffling their multicolored feathers against the wind, listen to the impolite yammerings of the geese, walk through the late summer kitchen garden and see what cabbages look like without their plastic wrappings, giggle at the billy goats and their private wars, admire the very unsleek, hefty-hoofed Belgians who so patiently tug the farm equipment, and think about life tied to the land, not the Beltway.

Then the question is not "How you gonna keep 'em down on the farm?" but "Why did we ever leave?"

Getting Down on the Farm
• *Claude Moore Colonial Farm at Turkey Run, 6310 Old Georgetown Pike, McLean, Virginia.*

Near the intersection of Routes 193 and 123, 442-7557. Open Wednesday through Sunday from 10 to 4:30. Admission. A 1771 12-acre farm, where the lower class, farm family prepares and eats a noon-day meal. Special programs from 1 to 4 on the first Saturday of each month.
* *Frying Pan Farm Park, 2709 West Ox Road between Chantilly and Herndon, Virginia, off Centreville Road, 437-9101. Open daily from 10 to 6. Admission free. Depicts a farm in the 1920 to 1940 period with draft horses, chickens, cows, pigs, and sheep, plus 15 acres in crops. Special tours available with advance notice.*
* *National Colonial Farm, Bryan Point Road, Accokeek, Maryland, 283-2113. Open Tuesday through Sunday from 10 to 5; $1 for adults, children 12 and under are free. Depicts a middle-class tobacco plantation. Holds a colonial funeral or wedding occasionally. To get there, take Beltway Exit 3A to Indian Head Highway, go 10 miles and turn right onto Bryan Point road, go 4 miles to the end of the road to their drive.*
* *Oxon Hill Family Farm, Indian Head Highway, Oxon Hill, Maryland, 839-1177. Open daily from 8:30 to 5. Admission free. Depicts a middle-class farm from 1898 to 1914, including horse-powered machinery. Special demonstrations each weekend (call for the schedule); visitors can often help with chores, collect eggs, milk cows, harvest crops. Special overnight workshops available with advance registration. To get there, take Beltway Exit 3A to Indian Head Highway, turn right onto Oxon Hill Road.*

SATURDAY'S CHILD

A CIVIL WAR TOUR FOR FAMILIES

"You mean they had a real war here? With guns?"

It's hard for children to believe that the Civil War raged even within the Beltway, on the streets of Washington and in the suburbs. After all, how could you have a cavalry charge down a freeway or a battle next to a shopping center? Here's a mini-tour to show kids some of the local Civil War hot spots.

To set the scene, you may want to start even before Fort Sumter. Go to Arlington House, the Custis-Lee mansion, whose white marble pillars and elegant but comfortable interior speak volumes about the antebellum South. Here lived Robert E. Lee and Mary Anne Randolph Custis Lee, descendants of Martha Washington. (To get there hike uphill from the Arlington Cemetery parking lot or take the Tourmobile; the house is open daily, 9:30 to 6, admission is free.)

Even from the Greek Revival portico of Arlington House, described by house guest Lafayette as having "the finest view in the world," war clouds could be seen on the horizon. In 1859, Col. Lee was dispatched by train to Harpers Ferry to recapture the arsenal from a band of 21 anti-slavery fanatics led by John Brown. The arsenal is still there, and you can tour the Master Armorer's restored home and get a sense of Brown and his raid from the exhibits and films at the Visitors Center, which is run by the National Park Service. (To get there, take the train as Lee did, or follow I-270 north to US 340 west to Harpers Ferry.)

The action reached the Washington area in July 1861 and was anticipated most eagerly by some Washingtonians who expected the war to be a cross between a picnic and a theatrical spectacle. Picnic hampers in tow, hundreds of Washingtonians drove their carriages down the Warrenton Turnpike to watch the first battle of Manassas. (You can get there by the same route, now called US 29-211 or via I-66 to the Manassas Battlefield Park exit; the park has picnic areas, so bring your basket).

The point of contention was a junction that controlled the sole railroad approach to Richmond. The leading antagonists were Gen. Irvin McDowell, leading hastily trained Union troops who stopped continually along the march from Washington to pick blackberries, and Gen. Pierre Beauregard, whose equally unseasoned southern troops nevertheless won the battle. Beauregard was aided by a group of Virginians led by brigade commander Thomas Jackson, christened "Stonewall" during the fight.

"There stands Jackson like a stone wall. Rally on the Virginians!" urged Confederate Brig. Gen. Barnard Bee. Bee died in the battle, and his grave is in the park at the end of a mile-long self-guided walking tour that begins at the National Park Service Visitors Center. The trail leads to the rebuilt Henry house, destroyed during the battle. Julia Henry, then in her 80s, refused to leave. She died in the house and is buried in the small family plot in the yard.

At most of the stops on the tour there is a recorded narration activated by a button, which even kids who know nothing about military strategy love to push. The recordings tell the story of the battle in the words of soldiers. In the Visitors Center an electric map illustrates overall strategy.

A second battle, equally disastrous for the north, took place at Manassas a year later, and you can follow the fight on a self-guided driving tour, which includes an old stone house used as a makeshift hospital.

What happened between battles? The answer to this question should not surprise a Washington child: There was a shakeup. McDowell, blamed for the Union fiasco, lost his command, and Gen. George B. McClellan tried to whip the recruits into shape. In the interim, a lot of battles took place away from Washington, and the Yankees suffered another defeat at Ball's Bluff, near Leesburg in October 1861.

Of all the ways to get to Leesburg, only one includes a house haunted by the ghost of the loser of the Battle of Ball's Bluff, Col. Edward D. Baker. On the night before the battle, the story goes, Baker dined at Annington, a private brick mansion on a hill plainly marked and visible from White's Ferry Road (reached via I-270 and Route 28 west).

At the famous dinner, Baker vowed that the next

night he'd dine "either in Leesburg or in hell." Baker, a senator from Oregon and confidant of Lincoln, died in the Battle of Ball's Bluff and, suffice to say, he did not dine in Leesburg. The Battle of Ball's Bluff is commemorated by a marker on US 15 north of Leesburg and reached via White's Ferry.

Going back across White's Ferry—which is guaranteed to revive a child's flagging interest in the war—you can introduce Confederate Gen. Jubal Early, for whom the cable-guided ferry boat is named. Early and his troops swept through the Shenandoah Valley, forded the Potomac somewhere near the present ferry crossing, and headed for Washington. On July 12, 1864, marching down Georgia Avenue, he reached Fort Stevens (at Piney Branch Road and Quackenbos Street, N.W.), the only fort to see action of the 68 that were built to protect the Capital from Confederate attack. Grant had rushed thousands of Union troops to Fort Stevens to thwart the raid, and the action that ensued is known as the Battle of the Suburbs. Washingtonians again thronged to watch the war—even Lincoln, whose head, towering above the ramparts, prompted Gen. Oliver Wendell Holmes to shout, "Get down, you fool!"

After two days of skirmishing, Early, who realized he was outnumbered, retreated. The Battle of the Suburbs is re-fought every summer, not at Fort Stevens but at Fort Ward in Alexandria (4301 West Braddock Road). Fort Ward features a map showing the locations of all the forts as well as a partially restored fort. The restored northwest bastion, one of five original bastions with a total of 36 guns, has replicas of the original guns, plus bunkers, a magazine, and a trench that originally connected Fort Ward to the other forts around the city. There is also an officer's hut, copied from a Matthew Brady photograph of the real thing, and a small museum.

My daughters, then aged 5 and 8, were impressed by the bullet shells in the museum and wanted to buy facsimiles from the museum shop (at 40 cents each). They also staged a mock battle in the earthworks, with "Gone With The Wind" accents. This led to a free-style rehash of the movie. The Cinderella coach in the playground near the bastion became the carriage in which Scarlet, Melanie, and the baby fled to Tara.

Like Scarlet and Melanie, women did their share in the war. Julia Ward Howe wrote the inspiring Battle Hymn of the Republic at the Willard when the hotel was housed in an earlier building on the same 14th Street and Pennsylvania Avenue N.W. corner. Less illustrious women and girls worked in arsenals, one of which stood on Fourth Street, S.W. At noon on June 18, 1864, some rocket shells were accidentally ignited and the Washington Arsenal, a hundred-foot-long wooden shed with a tin roof, blew up, killing 21 female workers. The women were buried in a mass grave at Congressional Cemetery (18th and E Streets, S.E.), and are memorialized by a tall marble monument. Lincoln and Secretary of War Edwin Stanton led the funeral procession, and the explosion—for which the superintendant of the arsenal was blamed—was proclaimed Washington's worst civil disaster of the war.

Other women, notably Clara Barton, were nurses in hospitals hastily improvised all over the city, even in the halls of the Capitol. When the Patent Office, now the National Portrait Gallery (8th and F Streets, N.W.), was turned into a hospital, office clerk Clara Barton got her start in nursing.

By March 1865 the north was confident of victory and the Patent Office became an elegant ballroom for Lincoln's Second Inaugural festivities. Lee surrendered at Appomattox Courthouse the next month on April 9. Five days later, while the city was still celebrating with bonfires and speeches, Lincoln was shot in the Presidential Box at Ford's Theatre (511 10th Street, N.W.), barely three blocks from the site of the gala inaugural. Children love seeing the elegant box where the dirty deed was done and older kids can learn a lot about the event and the conspirators from the museum in the basement. Lincoln died the next morning at the Peterson House, right across the street, a good place to end your Civil War tour.

ROSE HILL MANOR

Chief among a family's choices of things to see in Frederick, Maryland, has to be Rose Hill Manor, a historic home with a difference — at least 300 valuable, authentic items you don't have to keep your children away from.

At this Georgian manor, once the home of Maryland's first elected governor, little hands can crank the cherry-pitter, weave a row on the rag rug, wriggle into hunting shirts, and crawl up on a straw mattress.

To enhance your visit, we suggest you bring along:

A KID. Children under 17 are free to wander from the downstairs parlor-cum-playroom with a doll-house replica of the manor, 100-year-old rocking horse and dress-up corner, through the dining room where they can card and spin wool, weave a rug or stitch on to a quilt ("the boys really like that part," says tour guide Linda Tucker), and into the kitchen full of touch-me utensils.

A PARENT. Fourth graders and above, or those firmly under the thumb of a supervising adult, are allowed upstairs to see the feather bed (which you can climb into via stairs containing a discreet hole for the lovely white, ceramic chamber pot) and a 150-year-old desk with secret compartments.

A GRANDPARENT. Those raised in the Depression provide instant history lessons for youngsters in the kitchen. One spry, elderly woman on our tour groaned when she saw the cream separator. "My brothers were stuck doing that. I was too little," she said, pointing to the large gizmo that required 20 minutes of nonstop cranking. It was her husband's turn when we came to the old ice box: "The water from the ice melted into this tray, and we were always having to empty it," he explained.

Grandparents also seem remarkably tolerant when children discover the most popular item—a vegetable chopper with a pulley, gear and crank-run chopper blade that looks like the Industrial Revolution's answer to the guillotine and sounds like a freight train in a bathroom.

AN INFANT. Downhill from the manor house, in a log cabin rescued from a highway department execution and brought here from another part of the county, lies a wooden cradle with quilt all set for little ones. "Parents with young babies sometimes put them in here," says Tucker, "and you know, they go right off to sleep." Larger children (and adults) enjoy sitting on the rope-tied bed with its straw mattress and trying out the ladies' foot-warmer in this hands-on, one-size-fits-all home.

A NOSE. Out back in the herb garden, youngsters are encouraged to touch and smell the fennel ("smells like black jelly beans," says Tucker), tansy ("they used it like Raid to keep the bugs out"), mint, pineapple sage, and lemon verbena ("we make tea from these for school groups"). And they can admire the staff's monstrous pumpkins, broom corn (the stalks at the top were used to make brooms), flax (for linen), and squash.

A TEAM OF HORSES. In early November, "if the weather is perfect," says Tucker, most of the 20 or so carriages at a museum on the same grounds will be hitched up to teams provided by county farmers and driven through the city on the Historical Carriage Drive. The parade is glorious, observers say, but the fun part is watching them hitch the horses at the museum. Or you can leave the animals to imagination, and simply visit the museum with its hundred-year-old American, French, and Russian carriages and sleighs.

AN APPETITE. In early October, the manor runs a Fall Festival that includes children's games, craft sales, butchering (with sausage made and sold), and plenty of home-cooked food for sale. If you can't wait that long, bring your own fried chicken and use the long picnic tables near the log cabin.

SPARE CHANGE. In a smokehouse-turned-country store, there's a wide selection of inexpensive items custom-made for a schoolchild's budget: a wooden nickel (for a nickel), peppermint sticks, pens, and small craft items. There are also jellies, potpourri, mint teas and a few more expensive crafts and craft kits for those with money that goes rustle-rustle instead of clink-clink.

TWO HOURS. Tour guides suggest this as a minimum: one hour inside playing with the toys, textiles, and utensils; one hour outside touring the blacksmith shop, ice house, log cabin, carriage museum, herb garden, and country store.

Handling History

- *To get there, follow US 15 to Frederick, Maryland, Exit 8, turn left onto Motter Avenue, left again onto 14th Street, left onto North Market Street, and left at Rose Hill Manor Park. Admission for those over 17; free for everyone else. Open daily until October, weekends through December; closed January and February. For information, call (301) 694-1648.*
- *While you're there: all the historic district of Frederick should be interesting to children with lengthy attention spans or settled stroller habits. In addition, you might like to stop by Culler Lake-Baker Park, West Second Street at North Bentz Street, a nice place for kids to fish, or "The Golden Mile," off US 15 at Exit 6W, a strip of shopping centers and fast-food restaurants for families whose tastes run to burgers and fries.*

TROUT HATCHERY

At the Albert Powell Trout Hatchery, blessed events usually come 200,000 at a time. That's how many trout eggs arrive in one shipment—not via stork but via plane and truck, packed in ice and cradled in styrofoam.

"The eggs are shipped after they're eyed—you can see little black specks where the eyes are—which means they'll hatch a few days after they get here," says Roger Moore, manager of the hatchery, which stocks streams and lakes all over Maryland with trout every spring. According to Moore, 98 percent of the eggs produce rainbow trout that, after 16 months, are a foot long and

ready for fishermen to catch. The eggs are hatched in incubators in a small dark room.

"We try to make it like a natural stream condition," says Moore. "When a trout builds a redd—a nest—it's usually in a dark shadowy place."

About 10,000 pea-size, translucent eggs go into each tray in the incubation room, and constant 54-degree water flows around and over the eggs until they hatch.

"We come in and siphon off the egg shells with a glass tube attached to a rubber hose," says Moore. "When they've reached the 'fry' stage, after about ten days, we put them in troughs in the next room. They stay there, in the 54-degree water, until they're fingerlings. Then they go to the outdoor rearing ponds. They'll spend the rest of their lives in water that's about 54 degrees."

The water where the fish begin their lives flows from a limestone spring, the largest natural spring in the state, bubbling crystal-clear water into the hatchery's rearing ponds. According to Moore, the fast rate of flow keeps the water the same temperature all year round.

"I've fallen in a couple times," he says. "Feel it. It takes your breath away. In the winter you can see this place from miles away: mist rises off the ponds, since the water is 54 degrees and the air is colder. People always ask me if the water freezes in the winter. I tell them they can put it in their car radiators."

Workers in hip boots are cleaning some of the rearing ponds with long brushes. In others, six-inch-long trout dart back and forth in swift, constant motion. Kids lean over the sides to throw scraps of bread, which are fought over and quickly gobbled up. The fish also eat prepared trout food.

"It has 27 ingredients in it—fish meal and soybeans and things high in protein," says Moore. "When the fish are first hatched we have to teach them to eat, so we feed them ten times a day until they start to eat. By the time they get outdoors, they're down to three meals a day."

In the outdoor ponds, fish are arranged according to size. "We separate them with a grader," explains Moore. "The big ones stay in while the little ones go through. If we didn't separate them, the big ones would eat the small ones. Trout are basically cannibalistic."

In one large pond swim the real biggies—trout as long as 18 inches. These, say Moore, are the surprise bonuses for fishermen.

"These fish are two years old," he explains. "When we stock this year we'll put some of these in each stream. They're like icing on the cake."

Normally, fish are ready to leave the hatchery when they weigh about a third of a pound. They're put in tanks of spring water in the back of the truck, and the oxygen is pumped into the tanks. When the truck gets to a stream that state biologists say is clean and cool enough for trout, the fish are dipped into a net and carried by bucket to the stream.

"That's the toughest part of the whole operation," says Moore. "And the most important part. When we've gotten them this far, we don't want anything to go wrong."

The hatchery has had few incidents of human vandalism, but raccoons are a different kettle of fish.

"They just reach down and grab the fish," says Moore. "But our bigget problem is birds. There's a green heron around here that really eats a lot of fish."

As for Moore, he doesn't eat trout at all.

"I see them every day," he says a bit sheepishly. "I handle them every day. I eat haddock."

Heading for the Hatchery
• *The Albert Powell State Trout Hatchery is open daily, 9 to 4, (301) 791-4736. To get there from the Beltway, take I-270 to Frederick and I-70 west to Route 66, north for about a quarter mile to the hatchery. It's about an hour drive from the Beltway.*

AMERICA'S HIGH FLYING PAST

Imagine that you're in the cockpit of a North American F-100 Super Sabre, zooming away faster than the speed of sound. Twirling dials face you as you grab the stick, handling it like you've done it all your life. This is a single-engine fighter-bomber you're flying, so your mission is clear:

Get your picture taken.

If you've got a camera, the Smithsonian's Paul E. Garber Facility in Suitland, Maryland, can provide the cockpit at their annual open house in the spring. There, members of the public don helmets and goggles provided by the Museum and climb into two cockpit simulators, tour the nosecone of an elaborate Boeing KC-97G Stratotanker refueling aircraft, tie on a scarf and slouch jauntily beside Roscoe Turner's RT-14 Meteor, or pose behind an Apollo 11 astronaut cutout.

Or they can count bullet holes in Arthur Brooks' Spad XIII, the fourth plane the US Army lieutenant flew in World War I and the one in which he made his sixth kill. There are tombstones stenciled along its side, one for each kill made by the squadron, and holes ripped by bullets in the detached canvas wing. There's also a name stenciled on the side: Smith IV, the fourth plane Brooks named for his fiancee's college, "because they wouldn't let him name the plane for her, for some reason," says facility spokesperson Mary Feik.

That's in the shop (Building 10) where you're likely to find Feik, a gray-haired mobile library of plane lore who taught flying in World War II and worked as the first female engineer at the US Army Air Corps' Wright Field in Dayton, Ohio. She's been at work with some of the other 16 restorers employed by the Garber facility on a 1909 Wiseman-Cooke biplane, a delicate maze of wood, wire, string, and promise near the back of the building.

"We were surprised to find that instead of pieces of wood, they used laminated wood strips for the frame to increase the strength," she says with a grin. "We had quite a job of it. The glue (between the laminated strips) had dried, and we had to reglue each piece."

The wood enlisted by early designers for their planes was not always this carefully chosen. "We've found cigar boxes, parts of orange crates, cheese crates," says chief restorer Joe Fichera, a white-haired fellow with a blue baseball cap that reads "Waco" on the front, who started "hanging around airplanes" as a high school student in the 1930s.

"See this Ballanea?" he says, pointing to a restored 1927 high-winged monoplane in building 24. "We found what looks like orange crates used as struts," he says, pointing to a varnished wood strip that reads "Minneapo." "We left it like that—part of the original," he says with restorers' pride.

The craftsmen, mostly people "who love airplanes and work on them as a hobby even when they're not here," says Feik, run into, and around, a jumble of troubles trying to restore the planes.

"Take the Bleriot—that was a challenge," says Fichera, referring to a plane that has graduated to Air and Space Museum residence. "We didn't have too much information about that and just had to go on what the plane looked like. These old plane builders, they'd do something different with each plane. Nothing was standard," he says.

The craftsmen have designed parts from "fuzzy old pictures," says chief mechanic Harvey Napier, building parts from other parts ("you've got to measure first; it has to work, not just look right"), and called on help from around the country for their planes.

"This one had been covered," says Fichera, pointing to a 1912 Benoist-Korn, "with a rubberized fabric, so we sent a roll of the fabric to Goodyear. They build blimps and cover them with a fabric treated with latex, so we figured that if anyone could do it, they could," he explains.

They also store a "few space items," says Feik (an E.T. spaceship-shaped satellite antennae corrodes quietly in Building 10), "but concentrate mainly on planes, from a 1903 Wright brothers ship to modern day jets," she says.

Each plane is disassembled piece by piece, which accounts for the wings, bodies, floats, switches, engines, and zillions of gizmos and do-dads lying in well-arranged chaos around the shop. All pieces must be stripped of any corrosion, a task usually performed in a very off-limits area with yellow and orange chemical tanks filled with anti-corrosion brew.

"These people are practical people," she explains. "They don't necessarily have degrees in chemistry, but they've figured out how to remove corrosion in ways that are not at all straightforward." Once they decipher how to handle, say, metal corroded in space, they write up their methods for use by other restorers. "They are very much pioneers in this field," says Feik.

All metal and wood parts are covered with preservative, and any broken parts are repaired. "We'd rather fix a broken part than replace it," Fichera explains. "Our aim is to restore these planes, not replace them." That restoration may take as much as 27,000 man-hours of work, Feik adds.

Once the parts are put back together, the plane can be exhibited but not flown (because of the preservative). "We want these planes to last 50 years or more, but we won't know until then if we've done a good job," Fichera says, with no visible apprehension.

Each plane is labeled for the public, and at the Open House, restorers are available to answer "lots of questions," says Feik, and to help visitors into helmets, goggles and cockpits.

It's worth a mission to see them.

Getting There

- *The Paul E. Garber Facility's Open House is held in the spring; five buildings are open to the public. Tours are available by appointment at other times throughout the year; phone 357-1300.*
- *To get there, take the Beltway to Branch Avenue, head towards Silver Hill and turn right on St. Barnabas Road to Silver Hill Road, then veer left and go into their parking lot on your right.*

MARYLAND'S FARMS

What's black and white, says moo, and gives a thousand gallons of milk a day to thirsty Naval Academy midshipmen?

If you guessed the 450 Holstein cows at the US Naval Academy Dairy Farm, treat yourself to a glass of milk and a scoop of ice cream. On Maryland Farm Visitation Day, usually the last Sunday in June, many Maryland farms open their gates to visitors. The Naval Academy Dairy Farm is a regular on the tour.

"There are only 160 cows in the milking herd right now," says Lt. Bill Winstead, the manager and the only navy man on the farm. "The rest are calves or dry cows. A cow only gives milk for ten months after she's had a calf. On most dairy farms, calves are born in the spring, but we time it so ours are born in August, September, and October because it's during the academic year that we need the most milk."

The dry cows and the calves that have not yet produced other calves to meet the needs of the Navy graze contentedly on a grassy hill near the farm entrance. But the milking herd, says Winstead, never touches the green stuff lest one of them get hold of some sour grass. Instead the milk cows eat corn, alfalfa, and other grains grown right on the farm.

This being the off-season, there are only two calves in the calf barn. One just a week old, is sucking what looks like milk out of a quart baby bottle stuck through a hole in the stall. But, Winstead says, the liquid in the bottle is colostrum, the high-protein liquid the cows give just after birth of a calf.

"We collect the colostrum, then feed it to the calves through bottles for 30 days," he explains. But the weaning process starts early. The week-old calf is being tempted by a tray of protein pellets. A larger calf, already weaned, is licking salt block.

"Is that one a boy or a girl?" asks a child.

"We only keep the little girl cows," explains Winstead. "The bulls are sold, and other bulls are borrowed on occasion for breeding."

The milk cows—grown-up girl cows—are in the loafing shed, a shed and yard area where they relax between their two milkings a day, one at five in the morning and one at three in the afternoon. Toward milking hour, the herdsmen march them in groups of 16 to the milk house. While eight wait, the milkers wash the udders of the first eight and hook them up to the milking machines. In three or four minutes, about 23 pounds of milk has flowed from each cow through plastic tubes into a glass container hanging from the ceiling. While they're being milked, the cows munch on protein pellets.

"They're conditioned," explains Winstead. "They eat the pellets and they drop their milk."

Relieved of their burden, the first eight cows trot (maybe a bit more briskly) back to the loafing shed, and the milkers hook up the next group.

"We can milk 70 cows in a few hours," says our guide. "The milk goes through this pipe into a refrigerated tank in the processing room. We normally process after the morning milking. First it goes into the pasteurizer, then into the homogenizer, then into the separator. The separator is a centrifuge that takes out any impurities and separates the milk from the cream. These cows give milk that's 3½ to 4 percent butterfat. The academy wants milk that's 2½ percent butterfat, so the extra cream is made into ice cream."

Samples of the ice cream are one of the most popular features at the dairy farm's open house.

Visiting Maryland's Farms
• *For information on Farm Visitation Day and a list and directions to the farms on the tour, call the University of Maryland's Cooperative Extension Service, (301) 454-3712.*

FINDING FOSSILS AT CALVERT CLIFFS

Thirteen million years ago the place where we are standing was covered by warm shallow sea. The place is now called Calvert Cliffs State Park in southern Maryland. And as we shiver on the beach, we try to imagine whales, porpoises, and sharks swimming in the long-ago sea, and rhinos and three-toed horses running along the shore. For unbelievers, there is evidence: fossil remains of the defunct creatures piled up in layers in the cliff. As marine creatures died, they fell to the bottom of the sea. The remains of the land creatures sometimes floated down streams into the sea, too. Later during the ice age, the seas receded, exposing the fossil remains.

Now the cliffs are constantly being eroded by waves, and fossils often turn up on the beach. Fossil gathering on the beach is permitted, but digging fossils out of the cliffs is not.

Kids armed with spades, sifters and magnifying glasses are scouring the beach, digging in the sand and wading in the water. Paleontologist Tim Collins, who has brought a group of students to the beach, is called upon frequently to verify finds.

"Is this a shark's tooth?" someone asks him.

"It looks like a rock to me," answers Collins.

"Is that a shark's tooth?" tries another kid.

"No, but it's a piece of fossil barnacle," says Collins.

Sharks have about 300 teeth each, and there are a lot to be found if you keep looking. One girl finds a good specimen in the bank of a stream that runs into the bay, and the kids gather around to look at the tiny tooth.

"There are little places where the teeth attach," points out Collins. "That's one of the ways you can tell."

Another fairly plentiful specimen at Calvert Cliffs is the Chesapecten, a fossil scallop about 13 million years old. It's also possible to find fossilized oysters and tiny fossils of the turatella, a little animal that drills into shells.

Each layer of the cliffs represents a different period of time, explains Collins. When something new comes along, it lands on top.

To get the big picture of life in Miocene times, pay a visit to the Calvert Marine Museum in nearby

Solomons. There are Miocene mastadon teeth on display at the museum, plus peccary jaws, a rhinoceros tooth, and lots of sharks' teeth. The first collectors of sharks' teeth, says an exhibit, were Patuxent Indians, who turned the teeth into thumbscrapers or projectile points.

But at least one boy expresses the opinion the teeth were most formidable as weapons in the mouths of their original owners.

"Oh my gosh," he says, looking at an extra-large shark tooth in a case, "I wouldn't want to meet the guy that goes along with that tooth."

Fossil Finding
* *Calvert Cliffs is located five miles north of Solomons on Maryland Route 4. Admission is free. No dogs are allowed. To get to the beach and the cliffs, you have to walk about two miles down a wooded trail.*
* *Just so you know what you're looking for, it might be best to visit the museum first. It's on Route 4 just as you enter Solomons. The museum has booklets on the fossils of Calvert Cliffs on sale.*

LIGHTS FANTASTIC: BEACONS OF THE BAY

What was it like to live in a lighthouse? Anna Weems Ewalt grew up in Drum Point Lighthouse, a four-room "cottage" lighthouse that's now part of the Calvert Marine Museum. Then, as now, it was filled with antique rocking chairs, washstands, an old-fashioned Victrola, and china chamber pots.

The lighthouse, even at the time it was decommissioned in 1960, never had modern plumbing. A privy built out over the water and reached via the wrap-around porch, provided the sole sanitary facility. Water was collected on the roof and stored in the four 200-gallon tanks, one in each of the four main rooms.

"When my mother came to live here, Daddy went ashore to get her water," says Ewalt. "She wasn't going to drink any water that came off the roof. She was from Baltimore. My grandmother kept a horse and buggy on the shore, and some chickens. A lighthouse tender would bring kerosene for the lamps and coal for the stove. I guess it served all the lighthouses all the way down the bay."

The first lighthouse on the Chesapeake was built at Cape Henry before 1800. By the early twentieth century there were 74 lighthouses on the Bay, including 42 screwpile cottage type lighthouses like the one at Drum Point. Screwpile lights, the first of which was built in England in 1838 to mark the mouth of the Thames, were quick and easy to construct and suited to the Chesapeake's soft bottom. Unfortunately they were also easily toppled by ice floes. The light at Hooper's Strait on the Eastern Shore was found floating five miles from its original site in the icy winter of 1887, and the Pungonteague River Lighthouse, the first screwpile light on the Bay, withstood the ice only two winters before being carried away in 1857.

Drum Point Lighthouse weathered the ice and the years, its closest scrape with destiny being a summer storm in 1933 that flooded the cottage, washed away the boat, and forced the keeper to swim to shore. By 1960 silting had put the lighthouse practically on dry land and the Coast Guard, which took over the U.S. Lighthouse Service in 1939, replaced it with an automated beacon. Weather, vandalism, and red tape threatened to destroy the abandoned lighthouse, but Calvert County Historical Society finally steered it clear of bureaucratic shoals and found the money to have it moved to the grounds of the museum in 1975.

Like the Drum Point Lighthouse, the Hooper Strait Lighthouse, a similar screwpile cottage light, has also been moved to the grounds of a museum, the Chesapeake Bay Maritime Museum in St. Michaels. Also operated as a sort of mini-museum is the Concord Point Lighthouse, a 32-foot cylindrical lighthouse made of local granite, which stands in Havre de Grace, Maryland, near the point where the Susquehanna River meets the Chesapeake Bay. Decommissioned in 1975, the lighthouse has been restored and is open to the public on summer weekends. Also open to the public daily, if the foghorn isn't blaring and if Coast Guard personnel are available to escort visitors, is the Cove Point Lighthouse. One of three on the Bay still operated by the Coast Guard, the 51-foot stucco-covered brick cylinder is still a working lighthouse, a beacon to boats on the bay.

To the Lighthouses
* Calvert Marine Museum, follow Maryland Route 4 from the Beltway south to Solomons, a one-hour trip, (301) 326-2042.*
* Cove Point Lighthouse, take Route 4 from the Beltway south past Calvert Cliffs State Park then east on Route 497 to the very end, (301) 326-3254.*
* Chesapeake Bay Maritime Museum and the Hooper Strait Lighthouse, take Route 50 across the Bay Bridge to Easton, then Route 33 west to St. Michaels, (301) 745-2916. Admission.*
* Concord Point Lighthouse, take I-95 north to Havre de Grace and follow the signs to the historic district. The lighthouse is at the foot of Concord Street, (301) 939-1340.*

SETTING SAIL FOR THE BAY MUSEUM

The Chesapeake Bay Maritime Museum in St. Michaels, Maryland, has lots of things to appeal to kids—boats, live sea creatures, a play house that's really a lighthouse, and a big dog, albeit one made of iron.

"This is a little office," a mother explains to a small boy too young to understand the exhibit about the merchants who shipped the farmers' goods to the old world and sold them for old world luxuries, such as ribbons. "Is anyone working there?" asks the child, who likes the ribbons anyway.

"We're on deck," explains another mother to her child as they examine an exhibit on steamboats. "We're getting bombed," says the child, pointing to an old cannon on a ship in an adjacent exhibit of the War of 1812.

There's a life-size log canoe, just like the ones the local Indians made by burning a log and scraping it out with oyster shells, and a model of the Peggy Stewart, site of the Annapolis Tea Party of 1774. In the buildings and sheds spread around the sprawling grounds on the Miles River are bugeyes, skipjacks, and other workboats rescued from scrap heaps and lovingly restored by craftsmen in the boat shop.

But today the action is down on the docks, where the skipjack Rosie Parks is being hauled ashore for maintenance. A crowd has gathered to watch, but the process takes too long for the kids, who clamber up the stairs into the Hooper Strait Lighthouse.

Inside the wooden stucture, built in 1879 and moved in 1966 to the museum—without breaking a single dimpled-glass window—are artifacts of lighthouse life.

"Look, a waffle iron," says a little girl, who is dismayed to learn that the lighthouse keeper's family could visit for only two weeks a year but glad to hear that the keeper got frequent shore leave. There is less interest, for kids, in the exhibits of the history of fog signals—from bells to radio signals—and the Fresnel lens. But eyes widen again at the toilet facilities which hang over the edge of the hexagonal lighthouse.

" 'Cause, you know, it was in the middle of the ocean, so it would just go into the water," an older child explains to a sibling.

Outside the waterfowl building stands an iron Chesapeake Bay Retriever stout enough to climb on. The statue was cast in Baltimore in the 1850s as an advertising symbol for a company that made iron stoves. The breed it depicts descends from two Newfoundland puppies named Sailor and Canton who were rescued from a sinking ship and brought to Maryland in 1807. The Newfoundlands were bred with local spaniels and hounds. The resultant breed was recognized as a Chesapeake Bay Retriever in 1877.

The exhibit on the anatomy of a boat is complex, but kids are eager to try the hands-on "center of gravity" experiment. A piece of wood that's wider than it is deep is stable in a tub of water, they find, but it would be uncomfortable to ride on a boat shaped like a cylinder.

In a small aquarium eels, crabs, rockfish, and other Bay creatures swim in real Bay water, but the turtle that's supposed to be there is nowhere in evidence.

"Maybe something ate it," suggests a child who has obviously learned something about the ways of the water.

Setting Sail for the Museum
• The Chesapeake Bay Maritime Museum is open daily. Admission. For information, call 301-745-2916. To get to St. Michaels take Route 50 across the Bay Bridge and south to the intersection of Route 33, which leads to St. Michaels. Turn right on Mill Street to the museum.

ON THE BEACH, BY THE BAY

On a cinnamon-colored beach, hundreds of swimsuit-clad children, teens, and adults soak up the honeyed rays of the sun. A few of them wade into the breakers, where waves loom large to the three foot and under set, crashing around the knees of the tots' parents. In the distance rises the surreal outline of the Bay Bridge, a gigantic spider's web tugging trucks and impatient city folk to its shore.

The place is Sandy Point State Park, but its

beach scene could well be one of three other public beaches run by the Maryland Forest and Park Service along the Chesapeake Bay, or a beach of the dozen or so privately owned resort communities that rim the Bay.

A nice place for families, the Bay beaches combine the saltiness and wave action of ocean beaches with gentler tides, shorter drives and, in some places, fewer people.

But, as with any natural environment, the Bay also features some of Ms. Nature's nastier elements: sea nettles ("not fun," says Sandy Point's assistant manager, Gerry Thompson) and mosquitoes ("real healthy in the wilderness area," he reports).

Ouch. Why should people leave their nice, safe, close-by, chlorine-strewn pools and come here? "Crabs," says Thompson.

"A lot of people rent boats here just to go out and see the Bridge up close," he says, "and look for crabs around the pilings."

Then there are birders who tramp through the fire trails in Sandy Point's Corcoran Tract, a 130-acre wilderness area, and stalk the shores, looking for ospreys. Or boat owners who find the park's 22 launching ramps cheaper and easier access to the Bay than the posher marinas around Annapolis and Washington.

The park, in fact, fills up most Sundays by 1, its 2,000 parking places overflowing. "They'll stay in line outside the gate, waiting for someone to leave," Thompson says.

With nearly 535,000 daytime visitors last year, Sandy Point is by far the most popular of Maryland's public Bay beaches. "It's the most convenient to get to," says Barbara Rice, spokesperson for the Maryland State Parks, "and since it's right on the way to the ocean beaches, a lot of people know about it."

The same can't be said of Hart Miller Island, a site north of the Bridge that the US Army Corps of Engineers used as a landfill. It attracts over 140,000 people each year. "That's an amazing number," says Rice, "when you consider that you have to have a boat to reach it."

The 3,000-foot beach has roving lifeguards, but no facilities. "A lot of boaters like to go there, anchor, and swim," she says.

Boaters visiting or camping at Janes Island State Park, near Crisfield on the Eastern Shore, also like to row out to its island for swimming. The chief draw there, Rice says, is "fishing. Most people come to camp and fish." Big pause. "But there are BIG mosquitoes," she adds.

People come, not for mosquitoes, but for the bathtub races at Pt. Lookout, a park that tips St. Mary's County, where the Potomac reaches the Bay. "They have a little lake there," says Rice, explaining "and there's this whole class of people who like to modify their bathtubs so they can sail. It's a big sport."

The races take place in June. "We used to have them in September, and the weather always turned strange. It's quite a spectator event."

The Park also appeals to history buffs; it served as a prison for Confederate soldiers during the Civil War, a fact commemorated at the local Visitors Center. And for a fee, you can take an all-day cruise from here to Smith's Island, settled in 1657 and populated, the cruise people claim, with the original settler's 750 descendants.

Those who choose to stay on shore will find plenty to do on this, perhaps the most built-up of the Bay beach parks. Like Janes Island, it has camping sites, but some of Pt. Lookout's have hookups. Roving lifeguards protect the 900-foot beach, and bathers have access to a bathhouse and first aid station. Then, not surprising for a place with two waters, there is boat launching.

All the parks can be reached from one to three hours of easy driving—or sailing—from the Baltimore-Washington corridor, providing ready access to those who long to go salt water daffy.

Getting Beached

- *Hart Miller Island, managed by Gunpowder Falls State Park, Glen Arm, Maryland, 301-592-2897. The Island, located in the Bay north of the Bridge and close to Back River, has roving lifeguards along its undeveloped beaches. No facilities.*
- *Janes Island State Park, Route 2, Crisfield, Maryland, 301-968-1565. The furthest away, Janes Island offers camping, picnicking, rowboat rentals from May through September, and boat launching in addition to Bay swimming. Fees for*

entrance, boat launching, and camping; less for Maryland residents. Take Route 50 east to Route 13; turn south. Take 13 to 413; turn south, and go to the end.

• Point Lookout State Park, Scotland, Maryland, 301-872-5688. Located at the tip of St. Mary's County, where the Potomac River meets the Bay, Pt. Lookout once was a prison to Confederate soldiers. Today, it's a well-developed park, with a Visitors Center, family and youth group camping (including 26 sites with hookups), nature and campfire programs, boat launching and rentals, a fresh-water lake for fishing, picnic facilities, and lifeguards along the beach. Fees for entrance, boat launching, camping; less for Maryland residents. From the Capital Beltway, take Route 5 exit south past Waldorf and St. Mary's to the very end.

• Sandy Point State Park, Annapolis, Maryland, 301-757-1841. The most popular of the public Bay beaches, Sandy Point lies within perfect view of the Bay Bridge. Facilities include a bathhouse, first aid station, boat rentals, a wilderness area with trails, and picnic tables. Fees for entrance, boat rental; less for Maryland residents. Boat launching fee included in cost of entrance. Take Route 50 east past Annapolis; follow signs for park shortly before the Bay Bridge.

THE REAL, LIVE LITTLE PONIES

The real little ponies—not those popular pastel toys—live at the Land of Little Horses, in Gettysburg, Pennsylvania. About fifty of them, ranging from poodle-size to Great Dane-size, perform, let themselves be fondled, and take kids weighing less than 30 pounds for rides.

The guides emphasize that they are not freaks, not dwarfs nor midgets, but pure-bred Falabella miniature horses.

"Senor Falabella discovered the secret of downbreeding in Argentina. He was able to miniaturize these horses from standard-size horses and still keep good disposition and conformation, which you sometimes lose in downbreeding," said our guide. "The goal is not necessarily to get the smallest horse but to get one you can take a picture of with no one next to it and think you have a standard horse."

To illustrate, she took the horses out of their stalls one by one. There was Tommy, part Arabian and part English trotter; Peewee, an Appaloosa; Captain, part thoroughbred and part quarter horse. All were waist-high, but none had the stubby legs and oversize heads you sometimes see in miniature horses.

In the indoor arena, with crystal chandeliers hanging from the ceiling and bouncy artificial turf on the floor, the little horses proved they could do what big horses can do, and more prettily.

"It's a tough one, Don Juan," said the trainer. "Do you want to give it an eye?"

Don Juan, an Appaloosa in miniature, took the jump with style and grace, then progressed to the gate.

"The gate is 2 feet 3 inches high. This little guy is going to have to work pretty hard to get over it—that's what he says, too," explained the trainer. But Don Juan took it effortlessly, then put the whole course together and trotted off in triumph as flashbulbs popped.

The next performer was Sea Clipper, a three-week-old colt, who tottered in with his mother, Jezebel. First Sea Clipper nibbled on the artificial greenery around the jumps; then he tried to nurse.

"He hasn't had brunch yet," said the trainer. The foal then frisked around the ring and came up to the fence, where adults oohed and aahed and kids tried to hug him.

"It's all right, Mom," the trainer assured Jezebel.

"Watch your dress," she warned a little girl. "He's going to chew."

Then she picked up Sea Clipper, who weighs about 30 pounds, and carried him off.

Sea Clipper got his first name from the fact that the farm owners are former merchant marine officers. On a trip to Argentina, Tony Galuto saw some of the Falabella Miniatures, fell in love with them, and got to know breeder Julio Cesar Falabella. Galuto persuaded Falabella to sell him

50 miniature horses and, with two fellow marine officers, started the Gettysburg farm in 1970. The farm has an active breeding program.

"Senor Falabella developed the miniature to have a safe, gentle horse that children could learn to ride on," said Galuto. "He only bred the horses with good dispositions."

Most of the Falabella descendants at Gettysburg are gentle, though visitors are warned that stallions like to nip and that colts will teethe on anything handy. Stallions stay in a separate barn but many of the mares and foals are in corrals kids can—and do—crawl into.

"How long before they stand up?" asked a visitor, watching 6-day-old Laurie, who shares a separate barn and play area with her mother, Kim.

"A half hour after birth they're up and going," answered the guide. Even Sea Power, who weighed only 7 pounds and measured 13 inches.

At the end of the tour, the guide saddled up Carlitos, a full-grown miniature Appaloosa about three feet tall, and the kids lined up for rides.

"I've never ridden a horse, and I guess I never will," mourns a little girl told she's too big to ride. She brightens when told she can take a ride in a wagon pulled by a miniature horse around a quarter mile track.

These horses are strong—"because their hearts haven't miniaturized," explained the guide. "A miniature Clydesdale, for instance, can pull 900 pounds. We don't make them pull nearly that much, but at the end of the day of cart rides, we give them a glass of iced tea."

Hoofing it to the Horses
- *To get to the Land of Little Horses, take I-270 to Frederick and US 15 north to Gettysburg. Follow US 30 west for about three miles and watch for the farm sign on your left. The farm is open daily from April through October, and admission is charged. A snack bar and picnic grounds are available. For more information, call 717-334-7259.*

THE FAMOUS WILD PONIES

"Well, maybe this is just their bathroom and they live somewhere else," suggested 6-year-old Tabitha as she sidestepped what she euphemistically called "signs" of the famous wild ponies. We were on the pony trail at Chincoteague National Wildlife Refuge on Virginia's Assateague Island.

We had almost completed the 1.6 mile loop through the loblolly pine woods and even climbed an observation tower, but all we had seen of the ponies were these signs. Spending a fall weekend in Chincoteague, we hoped to see the ponies without the crowds that flock to the annual pony penning in July.

"Where's Big Bopper?" asked 3-year-old Caroline, referring to a nickname a *National Geographic* writer and photographer had given one of the ponies in a children's book.

My husband, who was striding ahead, suddenly motioned us to stop, and a small Sika deer crossed the path in front of us. A descendant of Oriental deer released here in the 1920s, the little deer leapt into the woods and stared at us inscrutably from behind a tree.

"I got him, daddy!" cried Tabitha, clicking her Instamatic triumphantly. Before she had time to advance the film, our real quarry came into view:

Nine horses and a young foal hurried across the path.

"Which were the Mommy and Daddy?" asked Caroline.

The daddy, we explained, was undoubtedly the stallion who was bringing up the rear. The mommy could have been any one of the mares in this typical wild-horse nuclear family.

The animals travel in bands of 3 to 20, according to Ronald Keiper of Pennsylvania State University, who has been studying the behavior of the ponies since 1975.

"There is rarely more than one adult male in a band," Keiper said in a telephone interview, "although there are some bands where two or three young males are co-dominant. Young male colts leave the band between their first and second years. One of the things I'm studying is what causes the animals to leave the band. Do they leave on their own or are they picked on by their father until they leave? I've seen young males picked on but never actually chased out."

Young fillies usually leave their parents, too, but not always, according to Keiper.

"I'm studying a daughter bred to her father who's produced an offspring," said Keiper. "So far the young animal seems healthy. Most young females may leave the band because of a built-in evolutionary mechanism that prevents inbreeding. The females aren't forced to leave. They leave on their own and eventually meet up with a stallion. There are some mares that I call liberated—they leave the stallion and wander by themselves. I'm also studying the relationship among siblings. I've been following three brothers. Two now have their own bands of mares, and one is in a bachelor group. I want to see whether they'll eventually fight over mares or whether they'll get along better because they remember each other."

The ponies, said Keiper, are so used to people that they don't mind being observed and go about their business as if no humans were around—once they figure out you're not going to feed them. The Chincoteague herd, about 130 head, is owned by the Chincoteague Volunteer Fire Company. Nobody feeds them—in fact feeding the ponies is strictly forbidden by the park service—and that's what makes them wild. They survive on their own, eating shrub leaves and dune and marsh grasses and drinking water from brackish ponds. Since this diet is low in nutrition, the horses are small—about the size of a Welsh pony.

Nobody knows exactly how the ponies got to Assateague. Legend says the original horses swam to the island from a shipwrecked Spanish galleon. A rival story claims they were exiled to the barrier islands when seventeenth century colonial legislatures enacted laws taxing livestock.

When we got out of the woods and off the pony trail, we saw lots of ponies. Some clomped along the road, causing mini-traffic jams to the sound of cameras clicking. Most grazed on the marshes.

Since our kids were tired after the 1.6 mile pony trail, we decided to do the 3.5 mile loop around

Snow Goose Pool by car. Known as the Wildlife Drive, the loop is reserved for pedestrians and bikers most of the day but open to cars in late afternoon. Edging past the serious naturalists who had set up sophisticated spyglasses to watch for waterfowl, we made our way around the fresh-water pool, pointing out herons, egrets, and other easily recognizable birds. For the kids, the highlight was a band of wild ponies grazing by the pond.

"Look at that birdie riding the horsey!" cried Caroline.

By way of explanation, I made up a story about how the bird had once found a foal who was lost in the woods and how in return the now grown-up horse gave the bird rides. The real reason, Keiper explained later, is that the egrets have a symbiotic relationship with ponies: The egrets eat the ticks, mosquitoes, and horseflies that pester the horses.

Meeting the Ponies
* *Chincoteaque is about four hours from Washington. Take US 50 east across the Bay Bridge to Salisbury, Maryland. Then take US 13 south to Virginia 175. Follow that route east to Chincoteague.*
* *Books to read to your kids before you go: The Island Ponies, by Barbara Ford and Ronald Keiper (Morrow); Misty of Chincoteague, by Marguerite Henrey (Rand McNally); The Wild Ponies of Assateague Island, by Donna K. Grosvenor (National Geographic)*

THE STILL ENCHANTED FOREST

We were winding through a dark passage in a caravan of teacups when, all of a sudden, the teapot that was pulling us stopped dead in its tracks. There was nothing to do but get out in what appeared to be a rabbit hole, complete with a life-size mannequin of Alice in Wonderland falling right into it.

"I hate to tell you, but they forgot to punch my ticket last time so you can follow me, because I know the way and I'm not scared," said a real little girl, leading us through passages with behind-glass

tableaux of playing-card people, the trial of the Knave of Hearts, and the Mad Hatter's Tea Party.

Alice in Wonderland, Ali Baba, Huck Finn, Mother Goose, and other storybook characters make up the permanent population of the Enchanted Forest, a vintage theme park near Ellicott City, Maryland, that many adult Washingtonians remember from their childhood days.

The characters live in thatched cottages, castles, and gingerbread houses set in a gently rolling woods complete with lagoons and a lake. Ducks and geese roam at will and a real rabbit inhabits the Easter Bunny House. There are several playgrounds and ten rides, all of them tame enough for toddlers. The attractions may be a bit too tame for the 8-and-over set, who see through the enchantment to the artifice.

"See, they use that light—it's called ultraviolet—to make the jewels look like jewels," pointed out my daughters' 8-year-old friend, Laura, as we cruised an underground cave in Ali Baba's Magic Mountain. My own children mistook the Middle Eastern setting for a Nativity scene, but Laura had heard the Ali Baba saga.

"You see, there was this thief and he cut this man up and put him in a sack..." she regaled as we sailed past a diorama about a blind beggar.

Fearing subterranean pallor, we surfaced for a ride in Cinderella's pumpkin coach.

"Bye, Miss Jackson! Bye, Miss Jackson!" chorused children wearing tags with the phone number of their daycare center. When the giant white mice and the pumpkin were filled with kids, the coach began its stately procession through the park and across the moat to Cinderella's castle, a three-story permastone structure.

There are antique cars to drive—usually into a fence—and a moon walk to bounce on and Huck Finn's Fishin' Hole to try your luck in.

"I saw one and it just went right past my pole," said a child, learning early the mystique of "the one that got away."

"Do you get to eat the fish if you catch one?" asked another child.

"Do you have to?" asked his friend apprehensively.

"Mommy, it's not working," said 8-year-old Tabitha, giving up fishing after a five-minute try and leading us to the raft ride to Robinson Crusoe's Island. This, in the Enchanted Forest, is connected by a foot bridge to Mount Vesuvius. While Little Toot cruises by Vesuvius, kids slide down the volcano and end up back on the mainland just in time to go on safari.

"We are now entering Jungleland," intones our guide as the caravan passes under a Trader Vic's type gate and into an eclectic, bamboo-and-poison-ivy rain forest, complete with elephants, a python, crocodiles, totem poles, and "natives" wielding tomahawks. Many of the ersatz animals moved. The baby elephant gave itself a bath. A crocodile attacked a hippo. Two monkeys shinnied up a vine to escape another crocodile.

"I saw the little thing that made them go up," said Laura, unwilling to suspend disbelief but enjoying it all anyway.

Meanwhile, back in Fairyland, Sleeping Beauty was just waking up behind a glass window in her castle wall.

"The prince is ugly," announced Tabitha.

"She's not so pretty either," agreed her friend. "She looks like Medusa."

For my 5-year-old daughter, Caroline, though, no ugly realities pierced the veil of enchantment. Wide-eyed, she pleaded: "Can we come back tomorrow?"

Finding the Forest
* *From the Capital Beltway, take I-95 north to Route 32 west, which leads to US 29 north. Follow 29 to the junction with US 40 west. Take that about two miles, until you see Old King Cole surrounded by handholding gingerbread men, on your right. You can't miss it. The Enchanted Forest is open 10 to 5 daily from Memorial Day through Labor Day and on weekends in April, May, September, and October. Admission. Food is available. Phone 301-465-0707.*

A WONDERFUL WATERFALL

"When the falls are falling on you it feels so...excellent," says a little girl.

We pause on a rocky plateau about halfway up Maryland's Cunningham Falls, which fall a total of 78 feet but do it in 220 feet of cascades, flumes, winding whitewater courses, babbling streams, and inviting pools. We're going the opposite way of the water on a climb where getting there is more than half the fun. You can climb all the way up on dry rocks, but in summer it's a rare climber who can resist the pleasures of getting wet. Clambering over the rocks, you can be at the top in ten minutes—if you don't stop to rest in every pool or stick your face on every cool, crystal spout.

A huge rock hangs above us, and the water takes various routes around, over, and under it. To the side of the main routes, in deep shade, a rivulet flows swiftly but gently down a mossy slide. We flow with it, sliding down about ten feet, then braking with the sneaker-heels-in-a-crag method. We could do this all day, but roars and gurgles above us promise other pleasures.

We come to another plateau where a dozen streams converge, and we manage to walk through all of them. Somebody's Labrador retriever joins us in the water, wagging his tail as he scampers out again. The main stream falls in a flat, broad sheet over a cliff. An offshoot pours out faucet-fashion between thick clumps of moss. To climb higher, we have to push ourselves up on a felled tree, then find a foothold on wet, slippery rocks. (Here my notes get a bit soggy.) There's an easy way around, through the hemlock and fern woods, but this is unthinkable now. We're committed to the water route.

The steep spot conquered, we're rewarded with a wide expanse of flat, lichen splattered rock that we immediately christened "the beach". Here's the sort of green glade Corot painted, the dappled sunlight

Gerard Manley Hopkins wrote poetry to, the crystalline pools the White Rock folks made commercials about. We take sandwiches out of a backpack and fill plastic cups with water from a natural spigot.

After lunch we bathe in a long, narrow lagoon of a pool, plunging in at the top and floating about 20 feet downstream, then climbing out and repeating the process. The water is cold, but the rocks are warm. We have brought no towels, so the children warm up in still, shallow pools heated by the sun. Butterflies flit by, and the afternoon wanes. We want to linger, but there's a primeval urge to be at the top. We follow the water through the woods, over a carpet of hemlock needles and mushroom spores. When the water's roar softens to a gurgle, we pronounce this point to be the top and head back down again.

On our descent we relive the pleasures of the climb up and discover still more pools to splash in. We're more daring now and even consider sliding down one of the steeper cascades. But when we ask a man who's sitting at the bottom of the cascade if he slid all the way down, his negative reply is accompanied by such vehemence that we come to our senses.

Once in the bottom pool, however—the swimming hole created by the final cascade—there's no holding back. We jump off a rock into about five feet of water and swim over to stick our faces into the waterfall. Just below the waterline is a rock made smooth by generations of derrieres. We take turns sitting on it, letting the falls tumble right over us.

My 7-year-old looks up at the falls we have just climbed up, down, and in and, with the skepticism of a generation for whom reality is defined by theme parks, asks, "Is this real?"

Disney himself couldn't have built it better, dear.

Cunningham Falls
* *The State Park is near Thurmont, Maryland. From the Beltway, take I-270 to Frederick, then continue north on Route 15. In Thurmont, take Route 77 west past the visitor center and the lake to the parking area for Cunningham Falls. The lake also offers good swimming, plus bathhouses and a snack bar.*